"David Boyd's book is the best I have read on cross-cultural ministry. Besides giving the biblical argument for having a multicultural local church, he also shares how one can grow a multicultural church in the face of the old-school missiological principle that only homogeneous churches grow. So whether one reads this to be equipped for the mission field or to grow a multicultural church, one's life and paradigm will never be the same.

"David doesn't just teach theory. He is a practitioner. I have been to his church. It may be one of the fastest-growing multicultural churches in the world with the most diverse cultural representation that I know of.

"This book will be revolutionary for some. As for me, it has provided tools to help me more effectively pastor Harvest Rock Church, a growing multicultural church in Los Angeles. It is must reading for any person who has a 'world vision,' which should be all believers committed to the Great Commission."

—**Dr. Ché Ahn**, senior pastor, Harvest Rock Church;
president, Harvest International Ministry

"When I learned that David Boyd was writing a book on multicultural churches, my heart leaped—just like Elizabeth in the Bible. Finally someone is doing multicultural ministry, not just talking about it. Multicultural churches are easy to talk about but hard to do! Discover the secrets of being in and growing a multicultural church in this book. David's work on the subject of the stranger is revolutionary.

"I heartily recommend this book. It's a book whose time has come."

—**Dr. Ed Delph**, author, *Church@Community* and
Making Sense of Apostolic Ministry

"David Boyd points to the increasing multiculturalism of the world's great cities as an opportunity to plant churches that will serve as strategic bases for mission to the remaining unreached people groups. No armchair theorist, David has planted a thriving multicultural church in Sydney. He writes from his own experience while remaining solidly rooted in the biblical pattern for mission seen in the book of Acts. This book should be required reading for all mission-minded Christians today."

—**Dr. Lorraine Dierck**, regional director,
World Outreach, South Asia

"I am told that writing and publishing one's first book is like having a first baby. When such a book is birthed from the heart, mind and pen of a close friend, one shares in the joy of birth that much more. *You Don't Have to Cross the Ocean to Reach the World* was conceived in David's mind years ago, and that seed has been watered and nurtured through the valleys and peaks of the lives of David and Chih Yunn Boyd. This is a book birthed out of experience. Not simply theory, it is more an insightful reflection on the Church as God intended it to be. As David points out, every church should be multicultural if it can be. There are lessons to be learned by all from this book. I trust you will be inspired to apply them in your own leadership and ministry."

—**Max Palmer**, international director,
New Life International

"Many pastors and churches today face a rapidly changing community filled with people of many colors, languages and cultures. Too often the reaction of the Church is to back away in fear or confusion. David points out in his book that God has brought the nations to our doorsteps. Never before have we faced such an exciting opportunity to build the Church and do mission in our own backyards. This is thought-provoking reading, and I recommend it to any pastor in a growing multicultural community. You will enjoy the inspiring examples from David's own church. Read this book and ask God what He can do with you and your church to impact the nations."

—**Tak Bhana**, senior pastor, West City Christian Centre,
Auckland, New Zealand

"David Boyd has provided us with a provocative and inspiring challenge about how to do missions. Every reader should find his writing thought-provoking and his anecdotal *sitz em leben* challenging to the status quo of missionary enterprise. His basic thesis is that bicultural practitioners are most effective in culturally adaptable 'coal face' missions, since their own life experience enables the enculturation of the Gospel with minimum personal culture shock. I recommend the work as an inspiring stimulant to the task that is ever before the Church. And knowing David personally, I can vouch for his wonderful work in multicultural Sydney. He practices what he preaches."

—**David M. Parker**, Th.D. (SCD), lecturer in
New Testament studies, Southern Cross College

you don't have to
cross the ocean to
REACH THE WORLD

you don't have to cross the ocean to REACH THE WORLD

David Boyd

Chosen

a division of Baker Publishing Group
Grand Rapids, Michigan

© 2008 by David Boyd

Published by Chosen Books
A division of Baker Publishing Group
P.O. Box 6287, Grand Rapids, MI 49516-6287
www.chosenbooks.com

Printed in the United States of America

Library of Congress Cataloging-in-Publication Data
Boyd, David, 1952–
    You don't have to cross the ocean to reach the world : the power of local
cross-cultural ministry / David Boyd.
        p.   cm.
    Includes bibliographical references (p.   ) and index.
    ISBN 978-0-8007-9447-7 (pbk.)
    1. Church work with minorities—United States. 2. Ethnicity—Religious
aspects—Christianity. 3. Multiculturalism—Religious aspects—Christianity.
I. Title.
BV4468.B695 2008
277.3′08308—dc22   2008004191

Unless otherwise indicated, Scripture is taken from the HOLY BIBLE, NEW INTERNATIONAL VERSION®. NIV®. Copyright © 1973, 1978, 1984 by International Bible Society. Used by permission of Zondervan. All rights reserved.

Scripture marked ASV is taken from the *American Standard Version* of the Bible.

In keeping with biblical principles of creation stewardship, Baker Publishing Group advocates the responsible use of our natural resources. As a member of the Green Press Initiative, our company uses recycled paper when possible. The text paper of this book is comprised of 30% post-consumer waste.

green
press
INITIATIVE

To my faithful parents,
Macdonald and **Patricia**,
who raised me and prepared me for life.

To my loving wife,
Chih Yunn,
who has stood with me through the challenges and
was willing to embark on this adventure of faith.

To my amazing children,
Nathan, **Peter** and **Amy**,
who had no choice but to come along for the ride.

I am blessed beyond measure to have a family
that stands together and whose top priority is
to be about the Father's business.

Contents

Foreword 11
Acknowledgments 15
Introduction 17

1. Focusing on the Forest 25
2. From Jerusalem to Antioch 31
3. Finding Bridges to Cross the Barriers 39
4. To Antioch and Beyond 43
5. The Rise of Hellenistic Leadership 59
6. The Bicultural Person 85
7. The Incarnate Principle of Mission 95
8. The Mandate Is for All 101
9. Our Emotive Response to Missions 107
10. Paul's Strategy for Church Expansion 111
11. The Stranger among Us 127
12. A 21st-Century Model of Missions 147
13. Case Study One: City New Life, Christchurch 161
14. Case Study Two: Jesus Family Centre, Cabramatta 171

Notes 191
Index 193

Foreword

The world's racial landscape is vividly changing. This is true especially in the Western world. As a new immigrant from Korea, my sister and I were the only children of color in our Maryland public elementary school. There were no other Asians, Latinos or African Americans. A recent visit to that same elementary school reveals great change with a minority white population. According to the 2000 U.S. Census, the percentage of people of color has more than doubled to 31 percent since 1960. And the acceleration of multiculturalism is expected to continue. The African American population grew by 30 percent in the last 20 years (1980–2000), the Latin community has grown by 142 percent and the Asian American population by 185 percent. In Los Angeles, where I live, there are now over 190 different languages spoken.

For the Church to ignore the demographic changes in the Western world would be sin at worst and total ignorance at best. For a church not to actively pursue multicultural diversity in a diverse community would be dishonoring to Scripture and dishonoring to God. Unfortunately, Dr. Martin Luther King is right that 11:00 Sunday morning is still the most segregated hour in America, and it is probably true in most of the Western world. In America today only 7.5 percent of the 300,000 churches are racially mixed.

The explosion of racial and cultural differences has produced an incredible tension within the community of believers. How should the Church respond to a multicultural society? David Boyd has given the answer to this question in his outstanding book *You Don't Have to Cross the Ocean to Reach the World.*

David Boyd writes in a clear, bold way that the church, when possible, should be multicultural. To support his thesis, he gives one of the most thorough biblical studies of the early Church showing that the Church was multicultural by design of a sovereign God for the purpose of reaching a diverse world. We all agree that racism is sin and needs to be repented of by the Church, but David does not approach multiculturalism from a justice perspective. He shares God's divine strategy that a bicultural person is best equipped to reach the world cross-culturally, and thus hasten the fulfillment of the Great Commission.

I have read many books on missions, always having had a passion to reach the world and also obligated to after having spent eight years of my life working on master's and doctorate degrees from Fuller Theological Seminary. David Boyd's book is the best I have read on cross-cultural ministry. Besides the biblical argument for having a multicultural local church, he also shares how one can grow a multicultural church in the face of the old-school missiological principle that only homogeneous churches grow. So whether one reads this to be equipped to go to the mission field or to grow a multicultural church, one's life and paradigm will never be the same.

David does not just teach theory. He is a practitioner. I have been to his church. It may be one of the fastest-growing multicultural churches in the world with the most diverse cultural representation that I know of.

This book will be revolutionary for some, but it gave me tools to help me more effectively pastor Harvest Rock

Church, a growing multicultural church in Los Angeles. This is a must read for any person who has a "world vision" where all believers are committed to the Great Commission.

Dr. Ché H. Ahn, senior pastor, Harvest Rock Church; president, Harvest International Ministry

Acknowledgments

Although this book has developed primarily out of the journey on which God has led my wife and me, we have been influenced significantly by certain people. Ed Delph from Phoenix, Arizona, has helped me to see things from a different perspective. It was Ed who encouraged me to write this book, and it was he who helped me understand how core values affect the church and its ultimate destiny. Dr. Ché Ahn also encouraged me to take up the challenge of the nations and inspired me to complete this book.

I want to honor those who have had significant input into our lives and have shaped our foundations. Without them this book could not have been written. They include the late Peter Morrow and his wife, Anne, who, as our pastors and leaders, have had an important impact in our lives with their love for all people, their heart for the whole Body of Christ and their passion for God. Pastor Max and Sandra Palmer cared for us when we came to Australia and were always a support and encouragement. Their vision for the nations has challenged our lives and kept us focused on the task. Graeme and Lucy Fawcett, whom we grew up with, have always been an inspiration and encouragement, with their focus and sacrifice for the cause of the Gospel.

Certain resources have shaped my thinking and given me an understanding of the culture and events surrounding Christian communities during the period when the book of Acts was written. These books include:

- *Annals of the World: James Ussher's Classic Survey of World History*, first published in 1654 and translated, revised and updated by Larry and Marion Pierce. Master Books, 2003.
- *Commentary on the New Testament*, by Adam Clarke, L.L.D. F. S. A. Clarke (1760–1832) was one of the most influential Methodists to follow John Wesley, and his monumental commentary on the Bible is a classical reference work.
- *The International Standard Bible Encyclopedia*, edited by James Orr, M.A., D.D. Written by a team of more than two hundred internationally distinguished scholars, this work was first published in 1915.
- *Missionary Methods: St. Paul's or Ours?* by Roland Allen—first published in 1962.

Introduction

As we look at the world community today, we can see three major trends that will have a significant impact on the direction of the Church and the issues it needs to address if it is to remain relevant in the 21ˢᵗ century. These trends are the movement away from the village to the city, the reduction of the population in the developed world and the movement of people from the underdeveloped nations to the economically developed countries of the world. These trends will significantly affect the Church, and unless it comes to grips with what is happening in the world today, the Church will miss one of its greatest opportunities for harvest.[1]

In 1900, 12.5 percent of the world's population was urban dwellers. A hundred years later, in 2000, this had risen to 50 percent. And it is predicted that by 2025, 64 percent of the population will be living in the cities of the world, and of this 64 percent over half will be classified as urban poor. The church of the 21ˢᵗ century must effectively reach the urban dweller; we cannot move forward in the task of the Great Commission unless we do this.

Declining birth rates and termination of pregnancies will shape coming world events. The population of Europe is in decline.[2] It is estimated that by 2050 the population of Europe, excluding Russia, will diminish by 75 million people.

Russia today is aborting over 50 percent of all pregnancies; approximately 10 million Russians of reproductive age are sterile because of failed abortions. It is predicted that Russia's population will decline from 142 million to 52 million by 2080, a massive 70 percent reduction in the population.[3] Japan is expected to lose 25 percent of its population by 2050, an estimated 20 million people.[4] Australia's birth rate is below sustainable levels; with fewer than two children per family, its population is growing only because of immigration.

Migration will radically change the face of the world, especially the Western world and those countries we call developed nations. From 1960 to 2000 Europe's foreign-born population rose from 14 million to 33 million, the majority found in the affluent cities of western Europe. As a result of Europe's aging population, and fueled by the declining birth rate, countries in Europe are turning to migration to help maintain a viable workforce. Germany, for instance, would have to receive 3.6 million immigrants a year to compensate for its declining population.[5] The United States of America is expected to reach a population of 400 million by 2046. Forty percent of this growth will be as a result of migration.[6] Australia's and New Zealand's economies are dependent upon migration, both nations having over 23 percent of their population born overseas.

The issue for the Church is that people are moving into the cities. The cities of the world are becoming multiethnic, with people from all over the world converging in these concentrations of humanity. They are looking for security and a future, yet the majority will be confronted with poverty and discrimination. The dream they are seeking will, for most, become a lost hope. Most of these immigrants will end up as a statistic classified as "the urban poor." It is in this world, created by the declining populations of the West and the move from the rural world to the urban, that the Church will face its greatest challenge, yet this very challenge holds the key to effectively fulfilling the Great Commission.

It is against this backdrop of world trend that my wife, Chih Yunn, and I, immigrants from New Zealand and Malaysia, started a journey that led us to Fairfield in Sydney, Australia—at that time the most multicultural municipality in the world. The journey began more than nineteen years ago when God gave me a challenge.

At the time I was pastoring a Chinese church with Chih Yunn in Christchurch, New Zealand. It was the first Chinese church in the city and was under the oversight of Majestic House (now known as City New Life).

As I was thinking about our future direction, I felt God clearly speaking to me. *David,* He said, *you can go anywhere in the world and plant a church, and I will put My blessing on it. You choose where you go.*

That started me thinking. If I were to plant a church whose success was guaranteed, I would surely want to do it in a place that had the potential to send out the Gospel in as many different directions as possible.

To understand this concept, it may be helpful to think of the seed head of the thistle. It opens up so the wind can blow the thistledown, with its attached seed, to a new location where it can establish a new plant. The thistle is dependent on the wind's direction to determine where its seeds will travel to, and on the wind's strength to determine how far they will be carried. Thinking of this diversity of direction and distance led me to consider three major cities as likely locations—London, Paris and Sydney.

London was a possibility because people from every country that has been part of the British Empire reside there. Paris was also possible because it is the hub for people from all the French-speaking colonies. Sydney was another option because people from every nation have come and settled within its borders. These cities all have the diversity and linkage that would make them influential in the context of spreading the Gospel. But as I thought about them it became obvious that, of the three cities, Sydney was the most logical choice for us. Moving there would be relatively easy, there was no new primary language to learn and New Zealanders at that time were given residence in Australia with all the accompanying benefits.

For a New Zealander passionate about missions, Australia was the last country I wanted to go to, due to the sense of rivalry there is between the two nations, and because I did not consider Australia to be a nation that needed missionaries! So I had to deal with some fundamental issues. First, there was the glamour of being a missionary. For many people who are interested in missions but who have not yet moved to a foreign country, the mission field can seem beguiling. Without realizing it, we can be as much motivated by fascination as by a sense of call. So my first challenge was to get enthusiastic about cross-cultural missions in a country that I felt was little different from my own. It meant I had to be concerned more with effectiveness than with any sense of fulfillment I might receive.

My second challenge was to recognize that mission was about people, not countries. A person's calling is not to a piece of earth but to people, whatever their ethnicity. We needed to refocus our thinking on what was important and realize that even though we were in a so-called "reached nation," we were still in a cross-cultural mission situation. Even though we came to this understanding, it was interesting to see the reactions from our sending church. Those who left as missionaries to go to developing countries (perceived as "genuine" missions) were given a high profile and good support. By contrast little support and profile were given to this church plant in Australia. Perhaps, too, we were not perceived as having the ability to accomplish what we felt God wanted us to do.

Our third challenge involved a new understanding about what mission itself was. It was not so much about sending people to the mission field as it was enabling the Gospel to move across cultural barriers and take permanent root in other cultures. This changed the focus from the technique of accomplishing the task to the task itself.

As we started to plant this church we took seriously Paul's comment in Romans 15:20: "It has always been my ambition to preach the gospel where Christ was not known, so that I would not be building on someone else's foundation." I felt God was telling us not to look at what He was doing in other Australian churches to determine what we should do. Our task was unique to our situation.

In Western culture, whether we like it or not, there is a strong drive to be successful. In the context of Christian ministry, success is inevitably measured by church growth, whether it be the size of your congregation, the number of churches you have planted or how much influence your ministry has if it is not church based. This pressure may induce us to adopt any new method that is having significant results overseas.

The first of these I can remember was the introduction of cell groups. This happened when Rev. Yonggi Cho's congregation in Korea was experiencing the outstanding growth that saw it become the largest church in the world. This ushered in the age of the cell group, with most churches in our part of the world adding cells to their program with the expectation of greater growth. In general the results were not as spectacular as had been hoped.

Other successful models that leaders have sought to adopt include the discipleship movement, seeker-sensitive churches, purpose-driven churches and now G12. But outside the culture in which these models were developed, they have had limited success.

So churches seem to move in cycles. As each new method hits our shores, either through visiting leaders at a conference or from the latest book, churches tend to adopt it either in part or in full. The vision is presented enthusiastically to the congregation, the level of expectation in the church rises and people get behind the program. Yet the results often fall short of expectations, and as one model wanes another comes to the fore, to be presented as "the new wineskin." So the cycle continues.

In time, as people start to realize that the new program is not working, they may lose confidence in the leadership. They may become reluctant to commit to new ventures and may even start looking around for another church!

As I thought about this oft-repeated cycle, which comes from the notion that if I have a successful method then I will grow a successful church, I began to realize that the life of a church flows out of its core values, ethos and culture rather than its methods. The core values of the church provide the environment in which God can move. If they do not provide this then, regardless of any method we adopt, we will not see the results we want.

This led me to the decision not to adopt the pattern of other churches. Rather, I determined to build the core values I considered we needed. We had to establish a church whose culture would allow people from a non-Australian background to feel accepted and whose ethos would build a vision for the nations.

This journey has led me to look afresh at the whole area of missions and how we do it today. It has helped me to ask questions of myself that I would not otherwise have asked. It has caused me to take a fresh look at the book of Acts and reexamine missions in the light of the journey we have undertaken.

When discussing missions I have tried to keep within what the Scriptures teach us on this subject. Much historical information has added to our current understanding of how we do missions. Jesus did many things that are not recorded in the gospels, yet the Bible contains all that we need to know about Him. In the same way God has given us in Scripture some crucial information about how the early Church expanded. Perhaps it is not the only way things proceeded, but it is the example God selected for us to learn from. Therefore, I have drawn from Scripture alone to present what I believe will become an effective model of mission for the 21st century.

I have reached the conclusion from reading the book of Acts that bicultural people were the ones God used to reach the nations and advance His Kingdom. In response to this the Church's responsibility must be to identify, incorporate, prepare and release such people to their calling.

The key to reaching the nations is first to reach the stranger who dwells among us. This gives us the opportunity to develop connected communities that can cross any political, linguistic or geographical barrier. It is along these community lines that the Gospel can travel and establish itself in totally new locations.

In the early Church, crossing the cultural barrier occurred primarily within the local church environment rather than out on the "mission field." The Church today needs to take back this role and learn how to build multicultural churches so the Gospel can move freely across cultural divides. The "bridges" are the bicultural people who belong to these churches. It is my contention that in the 21st century the measure of a mission-minded church will not be in the number of people it has going overseas on long- or short-term trips, but in how easily the stranger feels accepted in the home church.

As you read this book, it is my desire that you gain an understanding of the biblical keys that will help you become a part of a new 21st-century missions thrust.

one

Focusing on the Forest

When most pastors think of missions they focus on people, often those who have been sent out from their church. Or they think of the money they are raising to support a missionary or project overseas. Today in Australia much money is being poured into mission work, overseas projects and local missions. But when I listen to these people talk about mission, I doubt that many really grasp what it is all about. *We tend to focus on the trees rather than the forest.*

What would mission mean if we took both the missionary and the money out of the equation? For too long we have focused more on the method and resources required for accomplishing the task than on the task itself. But if we are really going to complete the assignment, we need to identify it clearly. So what exactly is this task to which we have been called?

> Then Jesus came to them and said, "All authority in heaven and on earth has been given to me. Therefore go and make disciples of all nations, baptizing them in the name of the Father and of the Son and of the Holy Spirit, and teaching them to obey everything I have commanded you. And surely I am with you always, to the very end of the age."
>
> Matthew 28:18–20

Jesus left us with the mandate to make disciples of all nations. The word *nations* here is a translation of *ethne*, meaning ethnic groups rather than geographical states as we understand them today. *Ethnos* is a defined group of people who have a common culture and ancestry binding them together in such a way as to give them a distinct identity. This identity is expressed in their worldview, common values, beliefs and behavior. These collective attributes distinguish them from those who do not belong. The degree of difference between ethnic groups is determined by the differences between their worldview, values, beliefs and behavior. These differences between ethnic groups may be defined as cultural barriers, a term implying a degree of insulation that protects an ethnic group from outside influences. The stronger the barrier between two ethnic groups, the less influence they have on each other.

If the mandate of Jesus is to make disciples in all ethnic groups, we would have to conclude that the task of mission is to transmit the Gospel successfully from one ethnic group to another. It must cross the cultural barrier in such a way that it becomes established in the new ethnic group and a community of believers is raised up that is self-supporting, self-governing and self-propagating. This church will contain within it all that is needed to bring redemption to that ethnic group. As I see it, the job of mission is half done when this community of believers is established, but it must be done in such a way that the essence of the Gospel is planted without the attachment of the cultural values of those who have brought it.

So, if we focus our attention on the process of transmitting the Gospel from one ethnic group to another rather than on the missionary, the money or the mission project, then one of the major challenges we need to address is the issue of understanding cross-cultural conflict and minimizing it.

Conflict of Cultures

If we see mission as the movement of the Gospel across cultural barriers, rather than as people going to another country, it would be helpful to take another look at the book of Acts from this perspective.

In Acts 15 we see a clash of cultures in the early Church, exemplifying the problem of cultural baggage. Antioch had been established as a church that was primarily non-Jewish, with multicultural values.

> Now those who had been scattered by the persecution in connection with Stephen traveled as far as Phoenicia, Cyprus and Antioch, telling the message only to Jews. Some of them, however, men from Cyprus and Cyrene, went to Antioch and began to speak to Greeks also, telling them the good news about the Lord Jesus. The Lord's hand was with them, and a great number of people believed and turned to the Lord.
>
> Acts 11:19–21

The church was well established and had already sent Paul and Barnabas—two of its leaders—out on their first missionary journey. Here we see the interaction between this multicultural church and the predominantly Jewish-cultured church at Jerusalem.

> Some men came down from Judea to Antioch and were teaching the brothers: "Unless you are circumcised, according to the custom taught by Moses, you cannot be saved." This brought Paul and Barnabas into sharp dispute and debate with them. So Paul and Barnabas were appointed, along with some other believers, to go up to Jerusalem to see the apostles and elders about this question.
>
> Acts 15:1–2

We see from this passage that the men from Judea struggled to distinguish between the essence of the Gospel and Jewish cultural traditions. They believed that to be saved you had to become "Jewish." This made for conflict in the church, since the fathers at Antioch were either bicultural (being from the Hellenistic Jewish community) or non-Jews. They had successfully established a non-Jewish church, and its members had even been called "Christians" by the unbelievers as they were so different from the Jews culturally. But when the monocultural men from Judea arrived they could not accept these differences, and they urged the believers to conform to their own values, beliefs and behavior. The resulting conflict eventually led to a delegation being sent to the leaders at Jerusalem to sort out the problem.

> The apostles and elders met to consider this question. After much discussion, Peter got up and addressed them: "Brothers, you know that some time ago God made a choice among you that the Gentiles might hear from my lips the message of the gospel and believe. God, who knows the heart, showed that he accepted them by giving the Holy Spirit to them, just as he did to us. He made no distinction between us and them, for he purified their hearts by faith. Now then, why do you try to test God by putting on the necks of the disciples a yoke that neither we nor our fathers have been able to bear? No! We believe it is through the grace of our Lord Jesus that we are saved, just as they are."
>
> The whole assembly became silent as they listened to Barnabas and Paul telling about the miraculous signs and wonders God had done among the Gentiles through them. When they finished, James spoke up: "Brothers, listen to me. Simon has described to us how God at first showed his concern by taking from the Gentiles a people for himself. The words of the prophets are in agreement with this, as it is written:
>
> > " 'After this I will return
> > and rebuild David's fallen tent.

> Its ruins I will rebuild,
>   and I will restore it,
> that the remnant of men may seek the Lord,
>   and all the Gentiles who bear my name,
> says the Lord, who does these things'
>   that have been known for ages.

"It is my judgment, therefore, that we should not make it difficult for the Gentiles who are turning to God. Instead we should write to them, telling them to abstain from food polluted by idols, from sexual immorality, from the meat of strangled animals and from blood. For Moses has been preached in every city from the earliest times and is read in the synagogues on every Sabbath."

Acts 15:6–21

Note the core of the Gospel, as identified by the Jewish leaders: "We believe it is through the grace of our Lord Jesus that we are saved, just as they are" (Acts 15:11). They recognized that the traditions, however valuable they were to the Jewish Christians, were not necessary for the Gentile believers. In other words, such traditions were not core Christian values and need not be carried into another culture. But the Jerusalem leadership did request certain practices to be incorporated into the non-Jewish church, for clearly stated reasons.

The Jewish community was found throughout the Roman Empire. The Jerusalem church leaders did not want the distinctions between the Jewish communities in the cities of the Empire and the expanding Church to be so great as to impede fellowship. If they did, it would also impede the believers' potential influence with these Jewish communities. So the whole issue was to maintain relationship, in this case with a rigid and inflexible Jewish community.

We can glean several valuable facts from this passage. First, cultural baggage can be attached to our Christian Gospel and go with it into a new ethnic group. Inevitably this creates an increased resistance to the Gospel message, as it is perceived as foreign. Second, bicultural people are far better equipped to minimize this cultural baggage. Third, monocultural people struggle to perceive the difference between what is Gospel and what is cultural.

In 2004 and 2005 we started to see a large number of East Africans join the Church. This happened because the United Nations requested Australia to accept some of the long-term refugees from Africa for resettlement. Many of these people were resettled in the suburbs of Cabramatta and Fairfield, and some of those who were Christians in the camps started to attend church. These people had been living for up to fourteen years in refugee camps where they struggled to meet the basic needs of their families. Yet even though they came from this background, it always amazed me that when the men came to church they wore a suit and tie! In fact, they were the only people group in the church who dressed in this manner. Where did this standard of dress come from? Traditionally a suit is not African dress. If we look back, we can see that this Western style of dress has become part of the Christian culture in Africa to such an extent that you would not feel comfortable in church unless you went dressed "properly," i.e., Western style. Even though these Christians were living below the poverty line, they still considered it important to dress in a suit when going to church. The Gospel has taken root in these people groups of East Africa, and along with it a Western value of dress has been attached. This value has become part of the unspoken requirements of those who follow the Christian faith.

These simple biblical and present-day examples highlight the blindness we often have as Christians and our struggle to see how our values and actions affect the process of crossing cultural barriers. As the book of Acts gives us a window into the world of the New Testament Church, let us look at how the Gospel moved out from Jerusalem and see if we can identify any key factors.

two

From Jerusalem to Antioch

Today we hear a lot about the importance of a biblical strategy for missions, and yet some of the concepts proposed appear to have little biblical foundation. Let us look at the E1 to E3 measure of evangelism found in the Lausanne 1974 International Congress on World Evangelism.[7] This is a way to identify the cultural gap between the community and the individual or team that is involved in evangelizing that community.

E1 Evangelism among one's own language and culture.
E2 Evangelism among people who are culturally near, yet sufficiently different to be unlikely to join the ecclesiastical tradition of the evangelistic worker.
E3 Evangelism among people who are culturally totally strange to the worker.

This is an excellent tool to identify how far away a particular person or group of people are located from our own cultural center. But if we use it to define different levels of mission work, we stray from the patterns that are illustrated in the book of Acts. Don't misunderstand me; I'm not saying what is being done in missions today is wrong. People are being saved and churches are being built, but I feel compelled to ask: Is there a better way for missions in the 21st century?

In my travels to Asia I have had the privilege of meeting missionaries from Western countries who have given up much to serve God in cross-cultural situations. I have nothing but respect for their sacrifice and dedication as they face the challenges of moving into a world that is foreign to them. While traveling in Vietnam with one of my Vietnamese leaders, we had the opportunity to visit a missionary and his family. As we shared fellowship I was struck by the enormity of the challenge that lay before this family. They had a new language to learn, a new worldview to understand and a new culture to function in. At the time I met them their lifestyle was very different from those they were reaching out to. Even though their standard of living was so much lower than what they had enjoyed in their own country, they still lived at a level that far exceeded those who were considered privileged in the nation they had come to embrace. These differences created barriers that hindered their effectiveness to incarnate the Gospel message, and they were unsure of the motives of those who responded to them as they were perceived by the local people as extremely wealthy. The stress and pressure that people have to live under in these major shifts in culture impact family relationships and relationships with others in a team situation, and they create an environment where success is the exception rather than the rule. E3 missions presents at best a serious challenge and at worst a recipe for disaster.

When I ask people who use the E1–E3 model in a mission context to illustrate an E2 or E3 example of mission from the book of Acts, I have only ever been given one example— Peter's visit to Cornelius's house. So all other examples of mission would have to be considered E1 evangelism. If this is the case, then we need to reconsider how we are doing mission and find out why the early Church was able to impact its world so effectively using only E1 evangelism.

If Peter's trip to Cornelius's house is the only scriptural example of E2 or E3 evangelism, we have a slight problem. Peter's prejudice was so strong that God had to give him an incredible vision just to get his attention. Then when Peter went to Cornelius's house he took others, not to help but to witness that he didn't do anything wrong. God had to move sovereignly on Cornelius's house so that Peter and the Jewish Christians would understand God wanted to save the Gentiles. We have here an extremely reluctant missionary who returned home quickly, apparently never to come back. Is this our model for cross-cultural evangelism?

To gain some key principles about reaching out cross-culturally, let us look at what happened in the first church and how the Gospel spread from there. We can see four directions of influence.

The Gospel Spreads to Judea

> On that day a great persecution broke out against the church at Jerusalem, and all except the apostles were scattered throughout Judea and Samaria.
>
> Acts 8:1

> Then the church throughout Judea, Galilee and Samaria enjoyed a time of peace. It was strengthened; and encouraged by the Holy Spirit, it grew in numbers, living in the fear of the Lord.
>
> Acts 9:31

These Scriptures suggest a movement of the Gospel away from Jerusalem, originally as a result of persecution but naturally spreading and growing in what would be considered the same ethnic group. This aspect of church growth was bringing redemption to the same Jewish cultural group. What had happened in Jerusalem was now spreading naturally to the rest of the Jewish community.

The Gospel Spreads to Samaria

Those who had been scattered preached the word wherever they went. Philip went down to a city in Samaria and proclaimed the Christ there. When the crowds heard Philip and saw the miraculous signs he did, they all paid close attention to what he said. With shrieks, evil spirits came out of many, and many paralytics and cripples were healed. So there was great joy in that city.

Now for some time a man named Simon had practiced sorcery in the city and amazed all the people of Samaria. He boasted that he was someone great, and all the people, both high and low, gave him their attention and exclaimed, "This man is the divine power known as the Great Power." They followed him because he had amazed them for a long time with his magic. But when they believed Philip as he preached the good news of the kingdom of God and the name of Jesus Christ, they were baptized, both men and women. Simon himself believed and was baptized. And he followed Philip everywhere, astonished by the great signs and miracles he saw.

When the apostles in Jerusalem heard that Samaria had accepted the word of God, they sent Peter and John to them.

Acts 8:4–14

As we look at the beginnings of the church in Samaria we find some other interesting details. First, the Samaritans were not of the same ethnic group as the Jews, but the two cultures shared many common cultural values that allowed the Gospel to penetrate with relative ease. Second, we are told specifically who impacted this community with the Gospel. It was Philip, a Hellenistic Jew. Third, it was clear

God was initiating this enterprise, as there were many signs and wonders.

The Gospel Spreads to Ethiopia

Now an angel of the Lord said to Philip, "Go south to the road—the desert road—that goes down from Jerusalem to Gaza." So he started out, and on his way he met an Ethiopian eunuch, an important official in charge of all the treasury of Candace, queen of the Ethiopians. This man had gone to Jerusalem to worship, and on his way home was sitting in his chariot reading the book of Isaiah the prophet. The Spirit told Philip, "Go to that chariot and stay near it."

Then Philip ran up to the chariot and heard the man reading Isaiah the prophet. "Do you understand what you are reading?" Philip asked.

"How can I," he said, "unless someone explains it to me?" So he invited Philip to come up and sit with him.

The eunuch was reading this passage of Scripture:

"He was led like a sheep to the slaughter,
and as a lamb before the shearer is silent,
so he did not open his mouth.
In his humiliation he was deprived of justice.
Who can speak of his descendants?
For his life was taken from the earth."

The eunuch asked Philip, "Tell me, please, who is the prophet talking about, himself or someone else?" Then Philip began with that very passage of Scripture and told him the good news about Jesus.

As they traveled along the road, they came to some water and the eunuch said, "Look, here is water. Why shouldn't I be baptized?" And he gave orders to stop the chariot. Then both Philip and the eunuch went down into the water and Philip baptized him.

Acts 8:26–38

35

This wonderful story shows us perhaps the first penetration of the Gospel into Ethiopia, an ethnic community that was culturally different from the Jewish one. Two cultural features stand out. First, God used Philip, a Hellenistic Jew, to initiate the contact; second, the Ethiopian had a strong connection with the Jewish faith and was possibly a convert to Judaism. Nothing more is said about this man, and there is only tradition to tell us more about him and his message.

The Gospel Spreads to Antioch

Now those who had been scattered by the persecution in connection with Stephen traveled as far as Phoenicia, Cyprus and Antioch, telling the message only to Jews. Some of them, however, men from Cyprus and Cyrene, went to Antioch and began to speak to Greeks also, telling them the good news about the Lord Jesus. The Lord's hand was with them, and a great number of people believed and turned to the Lord.

News of this reached the ears of the church at Jerusalem, and they sent Barnabas to Antioch. When he arrived and saw the evidence of the grace of God, he was glad and encouraged them all to remain true to the Lord with all their hearts. He was a good man, full of the Holy Spirit and faith, and a great number of people were brought to the Lord.

Acts 11:19–24

We are not told here who started the church at Antioch, except that they were men from Cyprus and Cyrene. This means they were either Hellenistic Jews or converted Greeks. We do know that Barnabas was sent to Antioch to help the fledgling church, and he proceeded to find Paul, another Hellenistic Jew, to come and help. So it can be inferred that Hellenistic Jews played a major part in establishing this church.

As we look at the spread of the Gospel from Jerusalem to Judea, and then to Samaria and to the uttermost parts of the earth (in this case Antioch), we note one obvious fact: In every case where it is documented that the Gospel crossed a cultural barrier, it was accomplished by a Hellenistic Jew. So the question arises: What was so special about the Hellenistic Jews that would cause God to choose them for this task of missions? To answer this question we will need to discover more about these people and where they came from.

three

Finding Bridges to Cross the Barriers

The Hellenistic Jews were an interesting people. To understand where they came from we must delve briefly into history. In 586 B.C. the Babylonian Empire defeated Jerusalem, the Jewish people were taken into captivity and many were resettled in locations throughout the Empire. This was a policy of the time, since displaced people were easier to manage than those who were left on their own soil. In 539 B.C. the Medo-Persian Empire replaced the Babylonian Empire. This change of rulership resulted in a change of policy. Cyrus's policy in 538 B.C. encouraged the Jews to go back and rebuild Jerusalem. Not all of them returned, however. Many had become wealthy and chose to stay. Over time these Jews spread throughout the Medo-Persian Empire and formed communities.

These communities were built around the synagogues that were established to provide an identity for the Jews and a place to teach God's Word. In 331 B.C. Alexander the Great conquered the Medo-Persian Empire and annexed it to Macedonia until his death in 323 B.C. After his death Alexander's Empire was divided among his generals, who ruled until the Roman Empire gained ascendancy. Through all these empires that flourished and declined, the Jewish people followed the opportunities available and spread to all the major centers of economic life, building communities that retained a distinctively Jewish flavor.

Wherever cultures interact, however, two things happen. First, they modify each other to some extent, with the minority group absorbing elements of the dominant culture. This made the expatriate Jews different from the Jews of Jerusalem and the surrounding area. Second, they developed the ability to understand Greek culture just as if they were Greek themselves. Hence they became known as *Hellenistic* (meaning Greek-cultured or Greek-speaking) Jews. We must remember that 83 percent of the Jews lived in the Diaspora (the area outside Palestine) while only 17 percent lived in Israel.

Knowing this background, we can appreciate the special bicultural ability of these people. They were bridge builders who could cross cultural barriers between Jews and Greeks with ease. From this we conclude:

- God prepared a bicultural people for the task of cross-cultural ministry.
- These people were bicultural because of historical circumstance and had bicultural skills before they were called for the task of mission.
- They all initially resided in the local church at Jerusalem.
- The Gospel crossed the cultural barrier in their own lives, in their home church, before they ever took it out to plant a new community of believers.

Thus the pattern of cross-cultural mission in the early Church differs from today's Church in several ways. Most of the people sent out to the mission field today come from a monocultural background. In the early Church they came from a bicultural background. Today people who are sent out are expected to develop cross-cultural ability on the mission field. In the early Church, God used only those with proven cross-cultural abilities. Today the cultural barrier is bridged on the mission field. In the beginning it was bridged in the sending church.

As I look at the people who have come to the church here in Cabramatta, I can see this principle of bridge building happening naturally in the church. One young couple in particular comes to mind. Yam and Binu are members of the Magar people; they speak Nepali and are members of one of the least-reached Mongolian people groups found in the foothills of the Himalayan Mountains. Yam came to Sydney in 1997 seeking work, and his wife, Binu, came later to join him. As they were exposed to life in a Western world, they quickly learned to adjust to their new environment and, because of their outgoing nature, they became at home in Western society.

This exposure to life in Sydney started them on a journey that would make them bicultural people. In 1998 Yam and Binu came to faith in Jesus and started attending the church. The grace of God was evident in their lives, and, as they grew, without realizing it, they were receiving the understanding of the Christian faith in an Australian context and then contextualizing it into their own Magar/Nepalese context as they lived in two worlds: their own Magar/Nepalese community and the greater Australian community. It has been interesting to see how effectively they and other Nepalese have been in sowing the Gospel in their community.

Today a large number of Nepalese have come to faith due to the effectiveness of bicultural people who first came into the Church. So even before any Magar people leave the Church, the Gospel has crossed the cultural barrier from the greater Australian community into the Magar/Nepalese community. Now it is not too difficult to move the Gospel through the connections of those in the Church to their families in the foothills of the Himalayan Mountains.

So what are the changes that might occur if our churches took seriously the mandate of missions as laid out in the book of Acts?

First, the main role of the 21st-century mission-minded Church would be to identify people who are bicultural and to create an environment where these people could be gathered and discipled effectively. Second, the 21st-century mission-minded Church must come to grips with the whole issue of becoming multicultural rather than monocultural. This would create a major shift in our current Church philosophy. To be involved in mission, the Church would need to change. Mission would no longer be an optional sideline only for a few in the church; it would become a core value of the church ethos and church life. It would not just be about giving money and sending interested people. The Church would have to move out of its comfort zone to create an environment where bicultural people would feel accepted and become stakeholders in its vision and leadership. A mission-minded Church would need to embrace a multicultural ethos within which bicultural people would be able to cross the cultural barriers personally. These people would then be able to transmit the Gospel into a new culture.

The mission Church would become the seedbed out of which the germinated plants could be taken and transplanted into the fertile soil of their unreached culture. With this understanding of the bicultural Hellenistic Jews, let us look again at the book of Acts and see what role these people played in moving the Gospel across the cultural barriers.

four

To Antioch and Beyond

An overview of the book of Acts from the perspective of the mission task ("the Gospel crossing cultural barriers") can be broken down into four main phases.

The Establishment of the Church in Jerusalem

For 33 years Jesus lived in the Jewish community. He grew with Jewish beliefs, values and behavior. It was from this community that He gathered the disciples who would become the leaders of the first Church. On the day of Pentecost the Church was birthed within the Jewish community, and its leaders were all Jewish. The Church was so Jewish in culture that, initially, Christians were considered a sect of Judaism. The significance of Pentecost was that it was one of the three feasts that were celebrated by the Jewish community, and both Jewish people and people who had converted to Judaism came from all over the Roman Empire to celebrate at this feast. This meant that when the Church was established people from both the Hebraic Jewish community and the Hellenistic Jewish community were present.

These two groups were so close that they could be considered one ethnic group or two subgroups.

It is interesting to look at the interaction of these two groups within the Jerusalem church. In many ways they were two separate communities living in the same city. Their differences can be seen in several ways.

First, they had different places of worship. The Hebraic Jews of Jerusalem and Judea worshiped in the Temple. We see that Peter went to the Temple for prayer, as was the custom: "One day Peter and John were going up to the temple at the time of prayer—at three in the afternoon" (Acts 3:1). The Hellenistic Jews worshiped in the Synagogue of the Freedmen. It was here that the opposition to Stephen occurred.

> Now Stephen, a man full of God's grace and power, did great wonders and miraculous signs among the people. Opposition arose, however, from members of the Synagogue of the Freedmen (as it was called)—Jews of Cyrene and Alexandria as well as the provinces of Cilicia and Asia. These men began to argue with Stephen.
>
> Acts 6:8–9

Second, they saw *themselves* as two different groups. The first church conflict was a cultural conflict. It was not just any widows but the *Hellenistic* widows who were being neglected.

> In those days when the number of disciples was increasing, the Grecian Jews among them complained against the Hebraic Jews because their widows were being overlooked in the daily distribution of food.
>
> Acts 6:1

So the first problem in the church was not an administrative one but a perceived discrimination between two distinct groups within the congregation. The issue was not that some

44

widows were being neglected but that the *Grecian* widows were being ignored. By implication those in the Hebraic community must have been having their needs met.

A glance at how the apostles handled the situation reinforces this idea of two distinct communities.

> So the Twelve gathered all the disciples together and said, "It would not be right for us to neglect the ministry of the word of God in order to wait on tables. Brothers, choose seven men from among you who are known to be full of the Spirit and wisdom. We will turn this responsibility over to them and will give our attention to prayer and the ministry of the word."
>
> This proposal pleased the whole group. They chose Stephen, a man full of faith and of the Holy Spirit; also Philip, Procorus, Nicanor, Timon, Parmenas, and Nicolas from Antioch, a convert to Judaism. They presented these men to the apostles, who prayed and laid their hands on them.
>
> Acts 6:2–6

The apostles considered this an organizational problem and responded by appointing leaders to take on this responsibility. It is interesting to note that all those chosen were from the Hellenistic Jewish community. This in itself indicates a separation between these two groups, as there was no need to appoint anyone from the Hebraic group, who were presumably well looked after and possibly already had leaders in place to fulfill this role. It is also interesting to note that the men selected were not just appointed as deacons, even though they were performing deacons' functions. Given that the leadership of the church up to this point was dominated by the Hebraic Jewish community, this was the first opportunity for the Hellenistic Jews to select leaders. We conclude these men were chosen because they were the up-and-coming leaders from within that church community.

When we look at the persecution of the Church, especially around the time Stephen was killed, we pick up some interesting insights into the Hellenistic Jews. The Hellenistic Jews who worshiped in the Synagogue of the Freedmen were less tolerant than the Hebraic Jews. They felt the same pressure most immigrant people feel today when they move to a new land—the pressure to belong. The fact that there were two Jewish communities in Jerusalem laid the foundation for them feeling like second-class citizens. Whenever this happens, those who are considered "second-class" may do one of two things. Either they will withdraw and live in their own world, not seeking any meaningful contact with the other group, or they will work as hard as possible to prove they are as good as the others.

Now let us look at the stoning of Stephen. When we compare Peter's message at Pentecost and Stephen's message in the Synagogue of the Freedmen, we would have to conclude there was little difference between the two messages. So why did Stephen get stoned while Peter did not? The answer lies in who was speaking and who was listening. Peter was from the Hebraic Jewish community and, even though he spoke to a group that was mixed Hebraic and Hellenistic, he did not incur the wrath of the Hellenistic community since his view did not reflect in any way on that community's perception of itself. But when Stephen stood up and spoke as a Hellenistic Jew to his own community, his words were too much to tolerate as they attacked their insecurities about their Jewish identity. Since he was one of them, they could not allow him to get away with these comments, as they would be perceived by the Hebraic Jews as not holding to the truth. It was this zealousness, fueled by a sense of being second-class, that motivated them to stone Stephen. It also motivated Paul's persecution of Christians that followed.

As you look at Paul's life, his early passion was to be the best Jew, a Pharisee of the Pharisees. This is all symptomatic of a person who feels inferior and is doing everything in his power to be recognized as an equal.

I myself have reasons for such confidence.

If anyone else thinks he has reasons to put confidence in the flesh, I have more: circumcised on the eighth day, of the people of Israel, of the tribe of Benjamin, a Hebrew of Hebrews; in regard to the law, a Pharisee; as for zeal, persecuting the church; as for legalistic righteousness, faultless.

Philippians 3:4–6

Stephen was a challenge to the Hellenistic Jewish identity, and his death was the result of their great desire to prove they were fervent Jews.

And Saul was there, giving approval to his death.

On that day a great persecution broke out against the church at Jerusalem, and all except the apostles were scattered throughout Judea and Samaria.

Acts 8:1

It should be noted that the Hebraic leadership was not touched by this persecution; this came later with the death of James the apostle. This would seem to imply that the persecution focused on the Hellenistic section of the church and was not a general rampage. It is generally agreed that if you want to destroy a movement you destroy its leaders. This was not the case here, and so the basic reason for the persecution was the zeal of the Hellenistic Jews for religious purity.

As we pull these facts together we start to see a picture of the church in Jerusalem. The church consisted of two distinct groups who lived within their own communities. The Hebraic leaders of the church released Hellenistic leadership to meet the needs that were found in their own community. However, there is no evidence that the top leadership of the church in

Jerusalem was open to the Hellenists. This meant that the portion of the church that had the ability to impact the world was not able to influence the church in Jerusalem to focus on the Great Commission. The marginalizing of the Hellenistic Christians in Jerusalem meant the impact of intentional church planting did not occur until they rose to leadership in Antioch. It is here that their values and passion could be expressed and a church of a different flavor was birthed.

The Spread of the Gospel within the Judean Jewish Communities

Two passages of Scripture provide insight into how the Gospel was spread into the Judean region—Acts 8 and Acts 9:32–43. These passages seem to show that the dispersion of the believers was initially due to the persecution that occurred after the death of Stephen. Having sought authority to purge this new sect known as the "followers of Jesus," Saul went from house to house arresting the people and placing them in jail. This led to people leaving Jerusalem and dispersing into the surrounding communities.

According to Scripture the believers scattered as far away as Samaria and Damascus. We are also told that God was moving in the communities they relocated to. We note two points from this.

First, only one person is named—Philip, a Hellenistic Jew. This would support the argument that this persecution was directed more at the Hellenistic Jews than the Hebraic ones. It also suggests the Hellenistic Jews were more willing to step out into new situations. They had already left their homes and come to Jerusalem. This meant they were more inclined to travel than the Hebraic Jews who tended to stay close to home.

Second, we observe the response of Peter and John on their trip to Samaria. They had heard what had happened, and so they went to Samaria, ministered and returned home. It seems at this time their focus was Jerusalem. They were ready to go out and minister when they heard something was happening, but after ministering they returned to Jerusalem. When we look at Peter's second journey, which took him to Joppa and then to Caesarea, we see a similar pattern. After Peter had ministered he went back to Jerusalem, which remained his base.

The spread of the Gospel into the surrounding Jewish communities was a natural extension of the church in Jerusalem. There was no need to cross any cultural barriers. The model we see of reaching the Jewish ethnic group is first to plant the Gospel in that ethnic group—this happened in Jerusalem—and then to build a genuine Christian community. After this the church can reproduce itself elsewhere among its own people. The process of community redemption was under way in that ethnic group.

The Crossing of Cultural Barriers to Three Different Ethnic Groups

We see in these early chapters of Acts the spread of the Gospel to three ethnic groups, apart from the initial Jewish ethnic group. In all cases the Gospel spread from the Jewish believers to people of other ethnic groups. Each action of God required a Christian agent to catalyze the process. The Gospel penetrated the Samaritan ethnic community and the Ethiopian ethnic community, although in both cases we are given only a glimpse of the process. The third community that was penetrated was the Greco-Roman community. It is this third group that the writer Luke focuses on. As he writes his narrative we can see both the process of cross-cultural penetration and the evangelization of that ethnic group.

In these three instances we find there are differences between the host culture and the target culture. Apart from the

Samaritans, these ethnic groups have different languages and different worldviews and values, but we could not claim that any E2 or E3 evangelism occurred, as those who penetrated these communities were all bicultural people.

The Samaritans were a people who had a similar world-view to the Hebraic Jews, and so the level of difficulty to penetrate this group was low. It is interesting to note that the first people to reach them were the Hellenists. It would seem that when the Hellenistic Jews converted to the Christian faith they had fewer prejudices than the Hebraic Jews. It was only when the news of the move of God among the Samaritans reached Jerusalem that the Hebraic leadership decided to make a trip either to confirm their leadership or to build up the new church community through the impartation of spiritual gifts and the ministry of the Word.

We are given little detail of how the Gospel penetrated the Ethiopian community. But we are given a glimpse of the person who carried this message to his people. That this incident is singled out and entered into the chronicle of the book of Acts in itself tells us this was a significant event. The Ethiopian had been in Jerusalem for a reason. The logical conclusion is that he was at least a seeker of truth. Jerusalem and the surrounding region were not significant in the Roman Empire. The only reason people traveled to this region was because of their interest in the Jewish faith. The narrative tells us he was reading Isaiah, which is in line with the conclusions we have drawn. That he did not understand the passage he was reading shows his level of understanding was limited. So he was probably either a new convert to Judaism or an interested inquirer.

We would have to conclude that the Ethiopian had a measure of understanding of the Jewish faith as well as an in-depth knowledge of his own people. This would possibly make him the best person to take the Gospel to his people. At least, it seems God saw it this way! Again we see that the bridge builder who took the Gospel to this man was a Hellenistic

Jew. The Ethiopian was a Gentile. When we compare Peter's reaction when God called him to minister to Cornelius, a God-fearing man, and Philip's reaction to the Ethiopian, we see clearly the difference in their perspectives.

The Hellenistic Jew needed only the prompting of the Holy Spirit for him to respond; the Hebraic Jew needed three visions to understand what God was saying to him. The Hellenistic Jew did not bring anyone to protect his reputation; the Hebraic Jew did. God did not have to confirm to the Hellenist that He was in this action by supernaturally moving on the people being ministered to; the Hebraic Jew, on the other hand, needed to know beyond doubt that God was at work. The Hebraic Jew had to return to headquarters in Jerusalem and explain himself, whereas the Hellenistic Jew just went on doing the job. How different they were in their ability to adapt to new situations. It all suggests that the Hellenistic Jews were better at extending the frontiers of the faith than the Hebraic Jews.

The Spread of the Gospel within Greco-Roman Ethnic Groups

The book of Acts focuses on the Greco-Roman world as it recounts the story of church expansion. The story begins with Peter's encounter with Cornelius. The next time we see God significantly moving on the Gentiles is at Antioch, where a large number of Greeks became Christians. After this Barnabas is sent, and his leadership shapes the expression and flavor of this church.

The story of Peter's visit to Cornelius gives insight into the apostle's apprehensions. He seems to need overwhelming guidance, and he fears criticism. God had to make the situation so clear that Peter had no choice but to accept the Gentiles' equality with the Jewish people.

Peter's involvement in reaching the Gentiles consisted of this quick excursion out of his comfort zone, after which he ran like a squirrel back to the safety of his hole. This is not the picture of an effective missionary; nor is it a model on which to build a theology of mission. However, on the positive side, Peter, by request, stayed with the house of Cornelius for several days. This meant that Peter considered Cornelius and his family as equals, because if a Jewish person did not he would not stay longer than a day in their home.

Now those who had been scattered by the persecution in connection with Stephen traveled as far as Phoenicia, Cyprus and Antioch, telling the message only to Jews. Some of them, however, men from Cyprus and Cyrene, went to Antioch and began to speak to Greeks also, telling them the good news about the Lord Jesus. The Lord's hand was with them, and a great number of people believed and turned to the Lord.

News of this reached the ears of the church at Jerusalem, and they sent Barnabas to Antioch. When he arrived and saw the evidence of the grace of God, he was glad and encouraged them all to remain true to the Lord with all their hearts. He was a good man, full of the Holy Spirit and faith, and a great number of people were brought to the Lord.

Then Barnabas went to Tarsus to look for Saul, and when he found him, he brought him to Antioch. So for a whole year Barnabas and Saul met with the church and taught great numbers of people. The disciples were called Christians first at Antioch.

Acts 11:19–26

At Antioch we see the transmission of the Gospel to the Greco-Roman world, where a community is built that could reach the rest of their ethnic group. This was catalyzed by the martyrdom of Stephen. We are told that "men from Cyprus and Cyrene went to Antioch and began to speak to Greeks also." This statement implies that they spoke to the Jews also.

For this to happen they would have had to be Hellenistic Jews, for mere Greeks would not be given room to speak in the synagogue. This suggests there was openness among the Greeks in this city. In fact, many became followers of Jesus, and their numbers were so large that they dominated the church that thus became the first Greco-Roman church. Some significant events in this story show the attitude and values of the Hebraic leadership in Jerusalem and the attitude and values of the new Hellenistic leadership that was developing and would soon express itself at Antioch.

From this passage we can infer as much about what is not done as about what is done. First, the narrative tells us that Jerusalem hears about the amazing move of God going on at Antioch. As is their custom, they decide to send someone to see what is happening and to give input. When God moved in Samaria they sent two apostles. When God moved in Antioch they sent Barnabas—but why?

Barnabas was not one of the leaders in Jerusalem. All we know about him is that he was from Cyprus. He was a Levite and had been in Jerusalem long enough to own land, which he had donated to the church there. As well as this, he had been instrumental in bringing Paul into fellowship with the leaders of the church when he returned to Jerusalem after his conversion. If, at this time, there were twelve men who walked with Jesus throughout His earthly ministry, why were none of them available? If today we heard of a great move of God that needed our help, whom would we choose to send? If we had twelve top-quality leaders, I would expect sending one of them would be the least we could do. It would seem none of these men were available to go, or they didn't see it as important enough to warrant one of the apostles going. Possibly the reaction in the Hebraic church to Peter's encounter at Cornelius's house had some impact on their reluctance to go.

This speaks much about the mission heart of the Jerusalem leadership. Their choice of Barnabas, who was not an apostle, to take on this important task shows how hard it was for the Hebraic Jews to step out of their own world. This rigidity had taken root in the Jerusalem church, making it ineffective in building mission-minded people.

When we look at Barnabas's response to the situation in Antioch, it is as interesting to consider what is not written as it is to read what is. Let us look at the situation. Barnabas comes to Antioch and recognizes there is more here than he can handle. He must find leaders to help. So what does he do? If you were Barnabas, where would you look for leadership? The obvious choice would be to look back to the sending church, as these are the people you know best and in whom you would have confidence. Interestingly, Barnabas does not do this. I think this speaks volumes about Barnabas's perception of the church in Jerusalem and how he perceived the leadership there. Why did Barnabas not look to home for help? I suggest that after he assessed the situation, Barnabas realized the leadership in Jerusalem would not know how to handle this situation. Moreover, if they were brought into this move of God, they would probably extinguish it by expecting the new converts to adopt Jewish ways. Possibly Cornelius's salvation was fresh in Barnabas's mind along with the accompanying reaction in Jerusalem. Barnabas's response was to find a man who had been nothing but trouble in Jerusalem. In fact, the leadership had sent him off to Tarsus for his own safety and that of the church. After that, we hear nothing about this man, as if he were off the scene and forgotten. Scripture tells us that Barnabas had lost contact with him and had to search for him. But why did he search out a man who had oppressed the church at Jerusalem and invite him into the leadership of the church at Antioch?

When we look at this man Saul, later to be called Paul, we see that at his conversion God had clearly spoken to him about his call to the Gentiles. He had gone into the desert, where Jesus had appeared to him, and there formulated the core of his Gospel, which would be the foundation for the Greco-Roman church.

In Damascus there was a disciple named Ananias. The Lord called to him in a vision, "Ananias!"

"Yes, Lord," he answered.

The Lord told him, "Go to the house of Judas on Straight Street and ask for a man from Tarsus named Saul, for he is praying. In a vision he has seen a man named Ananias come and place his hands on him to restore his sight."

"Lord," Ananias answered, "I have heard many reports about this man and all the harm he has done to your saints in Jerusalem. And he has come here with authority from the chief priests to arrest all who call on your name."

But the Lord said to Ananias, "Go! This man is my chosen instrument to carry my name before the Gentiles and their kings and before the people of Israel. I will show him how much he must suffer for my name."

Acts 9:10–16

I want you to know, brothers, that the gospel I preached is not something that man made up. I did not receive it from any man, nor was I taught it; rather, I received it by revelation from Jesus Christ.

For you have heard of my previous way of life in Judaism, how intensely I persecuted the church of God and tried to destroy it. I was advancing in Judaism beyond many Jews of my own age and was extremely zealous for the traditions of my fathers. But when God, who set me apart from birth and called me by his grace, was pleased to reveal his Son in me so that I might preach him among the Gentiles, I did not consult any man, nor did I go up to Jerusalem to see those who were apostles before I was, but I went immediately into Arabia and later returned to Damascus.

Then after three years, I went up to Jerusalem to get acquainted with Peter and stayed with him fifteen days. I saw none of the other apostles—only James, the Lord's brother. I assure you before God that what I am writing you is no

lie. Later I went to Syria and Cilicia. I was personally unknown to the churches of Judea that are in Christ. They only
heard the report: "The man who formerly persecuted us is
now preaching the faith he once tried to destroy." And they
praised God because of me.

Galatians 1:11–24

When Saul returned to Jerusalem, we are told he debated
with the Hellenistic Jews, and what he said caused them to
seek his death. During this time in Jerusalem, Saul probably
started to share his understanding of the Gospel with those
he came in contact with. Barnabas was one man who got to
know him and felt confident enough to introduce him to the
leaders in Jerusalem. Saul most likely shared with him his
heart and passion for the Gentiles as well as his understanding of the Gospel and how it related to the Greco-Roman
world. So Barnabas realized this was one man who understood what was happening and could move it forward. It was
this man he chose to be brought into leadership.

These decisions by Barnabas established the Antioch
church as culturally Greco-Roman, in contrast to the Jerusalem church, which was culturally Jewish. Antioch developed under a leadership that was predominantly Hellenistic,
in contrast to Jerusalem, where the leadership seemed to be
Hebraic. This meant the values and ethos of the Hellenistic
Jews came to the forefront in Antioch.

The Gospel on its journey from Jerusalem to Antioch had
crossed the cultural barrier and entered the Greco-Roman
world. This happened in the lives of those who carried the
Gospel to Antioch, in the sending of Barnabas and in the
selection of Saul. Men who were bicultural laid the foundation for the Antioch church to become the platform to
evangelize the Greco-Roman world. There is no evidence in
Acts that this church was involved in cross-cultural mission.
All who went out to the Greco-Roman communities lived in
the Greco-Roman world; they were either Hellenistic Jews

who were bicultural, mixed-blood people like Timothy or Greek-speaking people like Luke. The only person who was outside this Greco-Roman world was Mark, a monocultural Hebraic Jew, and he couldn't handle what was happening. Because of this, the churches established had essentially the same ethos as Antioch.

It would be a stretch to call Saul a model of a missionary. He did not cross any cultural or language barriers, and he traveled only within the Roman Empire. Yet Saul, above everyone else, understood what was required to plant the Gospel in the Greco-Roman world, and it was under his oversight that the Greco-Roman church grew and flourished, becoming the dominant influence and expression of the Church in his day.

From this investigation of the Hellenistic Jews in the book of Acts, it would not be wrong to conclude that these people were bicultural, had fewer prejudices and were more open and better equipped to extend the frontiers of the faith. If this is so, then let us look at the church in the book of Acts, where the Hellenistic Jews developed a place of influence, and see what impact they had on the development of the early Church.

five

The Rise of Hellenistic Leadership

When we compare the church in Jerusalem to the church in Antioch we see some interesting differences. As stated earlier, the real expression of the Church flows out of its core values, ethos and culture. So to understand the dynamics of these churches we need to discover what their core values were.

Jerusalem—a Church with a Rulership Mentality

Jerusalem was the first church—built on the foundation of the twelve apostles. Jesus gathered His disciples from a group of people who believed that, when the resurrection happened, the Spirit would return, God's rule would be worldwide and the nations would be gathered in. Their first focus was on the deliverance of Israel from all her enemies, establishing God's throne and ruling over the nations forever. This worldview was still apparent in the disciples even at the end of Jesus' time with them on earth.

On one occasion, while he was eating with them, he gave them this command: "Do not leave Jerusalem, but wait for the gift my Father promised, which you have heard me speak about. For John baptized with water, but in a few days you will be baptized with the Holy Spirit."

So when they met together, they asked him, "Lord, are you at this time going to restore the kingdom to Israel?"

He said to them: "It is not for you to know the times or dates the Father has set by his own authority. But you will receive power when the Holy Spirit comes on you; and you will be my witnesses in Jerusalem, and in all Judea and Samaria, and to the ends of the earth."

Acts 1:4–8

We can see here that Jesus was giving them the "Great Commission" to reach the lost, and His exhortation was for His disciples to be the agents of the ingathering of the nations; yet their focus was on the establishment of a kingdom in which they would rule. This was not the first time they had missed the focus and thereby missed the point. In fact, this whole concept of ushering in the new kingdom had caused problems among the disciples and led to competition between them.

Then the mother of Zebedee's sons came to Jesus with her sons and, kneeling down, asked a favor of him.

"What is it you want?" he asked.

She said, "Grant that one of these two sons of mine may sit at your right and the other at your left in your kingdom."

"You don't know what you are asking," Jesus said to them. "Can you drink the cup I am going to drink?"

"We can," they answered.

Jesus said to them, "You will indeed drink from my cup, but to sit at my right or left is not for me to grant. These places belong to those for whom they have been prepared by my Father."

When the ten heard about this, they were indignant with the two brothers. Jesus called them together and said, "You know that the rulers of the Gentiles lord it over them, and their high officials exercise authority over them. Not so with you. Instead, whoever wants to become great among you must be your servant."

Matthew 20:20–26

When this mother and her two sons came to Jesus their goal was to secure top positions in the coming kingdom. They believed Jesus was the Messiah and, as such, would soon reign over Israel, restoring her to her former glory. When the other disciples found out what they had done they were indignant, probably because they considered it unfair that others should get the top positions they felt they also deserved. We can only conclude all the disciples had this understanding of future dominion deeply ingrained in them.

Their second focus was on Israel, their own people. This monocultural mindset is seen in Israel and well illustrated in the story of Jesus cleansing the Temple.

On reaching Jerusalem, Jesus entered the temple area and began driving out those who were buying and selling there. He overturned the tables of the money changers and the benches of those selling doves, and would not allow anyone to carry merchandise through the temple courts. And as he taught them, he said, "Is it not written:

"'My house will be called
a house of prayer for all nations'?

But you have made it 'a den of robbers.'"

Mark 11:15–17

When Jesus cleaned out the Temple He was not solving the problem but rather exposing it. The Hebraic Jews were building a faith that was exclusive rather than inclusive. The need for religious merchandise required room, and so they

61

decided to use the courtyard that was reserved for the Gentiles. They no doubt thought this was the least important area, but it was the only place available for the Gentiles to come and seek God. That this was the only place that the Gentiles could come was never the intention of God, as it is clear in Scripture that the Gentile and the Jew had equal access to the Temple. While the Jews may not have intentionally excluded the Gentiles, we do see here an attitude characteristic of monocultural churches. They were completely unaware of how their values and actions affected people of different ethnicities. They did what all monocultural groups do without realizing it—marginalize people and lessen their sense of worth.

We see the same attitude in the disciples when Jesus talks with the woman at Samaria.

> "Do you not say, 'Four months more and then the harvest'? I tell you, open your eyes and look at the fields! They are ripe for harvest. Even now the reaper draws his wages, even now he harvests the crop for eternal life, so that the sower and the reaper may be glad together. Thus the saying 'One sows and another reaps' is true. I sent you to reap what you have not worked for. Others have done the hard work, and you have reaped the benefits of their labor."
>
> John 4:35–38

This passage is often interpreted as if Jesus were saying, "Do not look to the future but get involved in the harvest right now, because if you are always waiting for a future harvest to be ready you will never gather the current one." But while this is a great principle to apply, it is not what this Scripture is about. The disciples here were looking at a particular crop, which was planted but not yet ready for harvest. In fact, Jesus told them when it would be ready— in four months. The problem Jesus was highlighting for them was *focus*, not expectancy. Jesus saw that the harvest in Samaria was ready for reaping, while His disciples could only see the Jewish harvest. Because of their prejudices and lack of desire to move out of their comfort zones, they could not even see the ripe harvest in Samaria, let alone try to reap it.

Jesus' comment to pray for laborers also suggests a need for people who were not only *available* for a particular harvest but also *willing* to reap it. Their blindness was due to a strongly monocultural worldview, seen in their response toward Gentiles during their apprenticeship with Jesus. The following two passages illustrate this:

> Leaving that place, Jesus withdrew to the region of Tyre and Sidon. A Canaanite woman from that vicinity came to him, crying out, "Lord, Son of David, have mercy on me! My daughter is suffering terribly from demon-possession."
>
> Jesus did not answer a word. So his disciples came to him and urged him, "Send her away, for she keeps crying out after us."
>
> Matthew 15:21–23

The attitude of the disciples toward the Canaanite woman is clear. She was a nuisance to them. Her needs were of little importance, and from their perspective she was equal to a dog. This was the value system under which these men grew up.

> When Jesus had finished saying all this in the hearing of the people, he entered Capernaum. There a centurion's servant, whom his master valued highly, was sick and about to die. The centurion heard of Jesus and sent some elders of the Jews to him, asking him to come and heal his servant. When they came to Jesus, they pleaded earnestly with him, "This man deserves to have you do this, because he loves our nation and has built our synagogue." So Jesus went with them.
>
> Luke 7:1–6

Here we see a response of concern and benevolence toward the centurion, but the reason for it is clear. This man deserved Jesus' help because of his heart and action toward their community. Their response was conditional; he had been good to them and so they wanted to be good to him. It was not an open-hearted attitude to all people but a willingness arising from an obligation to someone who had helped them.

The culture of the Jewish people was strongly influenced by the Pharisees. To these people, being right was more important than life itself, and it was this attitude that Jesus attacked constantly. Scripture provides many examples: the woman caught in adultery (see John 8:3–11); Jesus eating with tax collectors (see Mark 2:15–16); Jesus healing on the Sabbath (see Matthew 12:9–14); and Jesus' disciples eating grain they harvested on the Sabbath (see Matthew 12:1–2).

Core Values of the Jerusalem Church

The expression and direction of a church is molded by its leadership, and Jerusalem was no exception. Many core values are apparent in this church, but I want to deal here with those that pertain to its mission to reach the world.

Strict observance of the Law had become a core value for the Hebraic Jews, and when Jesus challenged this value He drew a sharp reaction from the Pharisees. Even the disciples, who had walked with Jesus for two or three years, had not fully dealt with these issues, as we see from the story of the woman at the well. They were astonished to see Jesus talking to a woman, and a Samaritan at that. Here, issues of right and wrong were more important to them than life and death.

As we proceed to look at the church in Jerusalem, we will see how these core values influenced the expression of the church and ultimately determined its effectiveness or the lack thereof.

The Background of the Jerusalem Church

The Jerusalem church was birthed in revival, and great things were happening. People were focused on community, and there was a commitment to one another and to the purposes of God. The supernatural was in evidence, people were being saved daily, the growing Church had good leadership and believers were enjoying what God was doing in the city.

> Those who accepted his message were baptized, and about three thousand were added to their number that day.
>
> They devoted themselves to the apostles' teaching and to the fellowship, to the breaking of bread and to prayer. Everyone was filled with awe, and many wonders and miraculous signs were done by the apostles. All the believers were together and had everything in common. Selling their possessions and goods, they gave to anyone as he had need. Every day they continued to meet together in the temple courts. They broke bread in their homes and ate together with glad and sincere hearts, praising God and enjoying the favor of all the people. And the Lord added to their number daily those who were being saved.
>
> Acts 2:41–47

A dynamic was operating that most modern churches would envy: the ongoing, visible work of God. The Holy Spirit was working with many signs and wonders, and there were occasions when even the very shadows of some of the apostles touching the sick were enough to heal them. The apostles were seeing the ministry of Jesus expressed through their own. God was declaring His rulership over the Church, not only exposing sin but also dealing with it. (The story of Ananias and Sapphira was a case in point.)

65

The Church's response to this was to build community—in such a way that the members remained strongly attached to it. "They devoted themselves to the apostles' teaching and to fellowship, to the breaking of bread and to prayer," four activities that this early Church saw as fundamental to its life.

It is interesting that two of the four activities—fellowship and sharing a meal together—are focused on building relationships. Out of this connectedness in relationship was a genuine sharing of their material wealth.

The Church did not develop a compulsory communal lifestyle. Ananias and Sapphira, for example, owned their land and had every right to do what they wished with it.

> Now a man named Ananias, together with his wife Sapphira, also sold a piece of property. With his wife's full knowledge he kept back part of the money for himself, but brought the rest and put it at the apostles' feet.
>
> Then Peter said, "Ananias, how is it that Satan has so filled your heart that you have lied to the Holy Spirit and have kept for yourself some of the money you received for the land? Didn't it belong to you before it was sold? And after it was sold, wasn't the money at your disposal? What made you think of doing such a thing? You have not lied to men but to God."
>
> Acts 5:1–4

The sharing in common was based on a foundation of relationship, which flowed into caring and sharing. When this becomes organized and leaders exert pressure on people to bring them into what is "a good thing," we move from a response of grace to a work of law. We also risk building a cult mentality.

It is of interest to note that it is only in Jerusalem that we have this distribution of wealth and sharing to those in need so visibly identified. This shows us that there were a large number of people from the "Jews of the Dispersion" who were converted and remained in Jerusalem for some time. It was not the locals who lacked resources to live, as they had an established means of livelihood. Those who were saved at Pentecost from outside of Jerusalem had no means of support and needed the financial support of the community while they grew in their newfound faith.

The dynamics of this church and the sense of excitement as they watched God moving constantly within their community would have powerfully motivated the people to remain in Jerusalem. To fulfill the mandate to go into all ethnic groups and plant the church, they would need either intentional direction or persecution.

So how did a church with such dynamics fail to make a significant impact in its generation? The answer lies in its core values and how they worked themselves out in the leadership.

The Focus on Ruling

First, the church in Jerusalem did not focus on reaching the nations. Since the apostles believed Jesus was coming to rule and reign from Jerusalem, they were not particularly interested in leaving that city. And when they did go out they quickly returned to the place where everything was supposed to be happening. We see this in Peter's visit to Samaria and to the house of Cornelius. As soon as the job was done he returned to Jerusalem. It is hard to reach the world when one's focus is on a specific location.

Second, they focused on the Jewish people. Peter himself said he felt called to reach the Jews, whereas he saw Paul called to reach the Gentiles (in other words, all the others). It is interesting to note in Galatians 2:9 that James, Peter and John perceived their call to be only to the Jews despite Jesus saying in Matthew 28 that they were to go to all nations and make disciples. This exemplifies an incompatibility between the clear teaching of Jesus and the Church's core values, and when these are in conflict the core values predominate.

> As for those who seemed to be important—whatever they were makes no difference to me; God does not judge by external appearance—those men added nothing to my message. On the contrary, they saw that I had been entrusted with the task of preaching the gospel to the Gentiles, just as Peter had been to the Jews. For God, who was at work in the ministry of Peter as an apostle to the Jews, was also at work in my ministry as an apostle to the Gentiles. James, Peter and John, those reputed to be pillars, gave me and Barnabas the right hand of fellowship when they recognized the grace given to me. They agreed that we should go to the Gentiles, and they to the Jews. All they asked was that we should continue to remember the poor, the very thing I was eager to do.
>
> Galatians 2:6–10

The church stayed with what they knew and felt comfortable with; it did not intentionally build a leadership team that would change this monocultural mindset, perhaps because the need to do so never occurred to them.

We can see from their core values that the Jerusalem church could not develop an intentional mission strategy. As we look at the development of the early Church, up to the sending out of missionaries from Antioch, we see the leaders responding to what God had already done, rather than being carriers of the vision and setting out to fulfill the mandate. The first breakout from Jerusalem came from a persecution that forced the people to leave, and this dispersion unintentionally started the spread of the Gospel.

When God moved in an area such as Samaria, the leaders at Jerusalem responded by sending a delegate of leaders there both to give input and to establish a link with this fledgling

Christian community. However, they quickly headed back to Jerusalem. Peter's ministry to Cornelius, discussed in chapters 2 and 4, shows clearly the reluctance or inability of this church to participate in missions.

When revival broke out in Antioch, the church in Jerusalem sent Barnabas to check it out. The fact the church sent someone who lacked influence in Jerusalem, and Barnabas's own lack of response to Jerusalem after assessing the situation at Antioch, reinforces our picture of Jerusalem as a church with only a token response to missions. This church saw its mandate as building and containing the revival in Jerusalem, rather than fulfilling the commission of Jesus to go into the entire world and preach the Gospel.

A Church That Was Inflexible

One consequence of monoculturalism was an apparent lack of flexibility in the Jerusalem church. We see this when some of the leaders from Antioch come to Jerusalem to solve a dispute between the two churches. This seems to be an interchurch dispute, since the Jerusalem leadership did not appear to have authority over the other churches. If it did, it would have sent edicts to all the churches stating "how things were going to be," and many of the issues Paul discusses in his letters would not have needed to be addressed. (He deals in principle with the issues that came up through this dispute in Antioch.) But Paul did not quote any edict from the Jerusalem church and say "case closed." This suggests that the situation was possibly a difficulty between these two churches. This issue was dealt with on a church-by-church basis.

When we look at the resolution of this conflict we see an interesting attitude on the part of the leaders in Jerusalem. Basically, they suggested the Gentiles needed to change so the Jews could have fellowship with them.

"Now then, why do you try to test God by putting on the necks of the disciples a yoke that neither we nor our fathers have been able to bear? No! We believe it is through the grace of our Lord Jesus that we are saved, just as they are. . . . It is my judgment, therefore, that we should not make it difficult for the Gentiles who are turning to God. Instead we should write to them, telling them to abstain from food polluted by idols, from sexual immorality, from the meat of strangled animals and from blood. For Moses has been preached in every city from the earliest times and is read in the synagogues on every Sabbath."

Acts 15:10–11, 19–21

The leaders clearly understood that all were saved by grace. So why did they expect the Gentiles to keep certain laws? It was not because some laws were more important than others; nor was Christianity a religion of grace "plus some laws." The reason given was that if the Gentiles did not do this, then the Jews could not fellowship with them. In that culture, the Jews would not consider having fellowship with Gentiles because of the Gentiles' lifestyle. Any Gentile involved in practices such as those addressed in Acts 15 would be excluded from fellowship with any Jewish person.

Because we live in a 21st-century world with different values than the first century, we possibly cannot understand this conclusion. The only comparison I can give is to look at Westerners' reaction to eating dog meat. Westerners would not eat a dog even if they were extremely hungry. It is so ingrained in them that to eat a dog is wrong that they do not have to explain it. However, people in Vietnam or Korea would have a hard time understanding that reaction or reasoning, as their view on eating dog is so different. Similarly, the exclusion of the Gentiles from fellowship with the Jews because of their lifestyle was so fundamental in the first-century Jewish world that it would not be explained, as those involved would automatically understand the reason.

The issue here in Acts was one of maintaining unity, a notion which itself is good. However, what is interesting is that the Jerusalem church put the requirement for unity on the shoulders of the Gentiles! There was no indication the Jewish Christians realized a need to change. Rather, the Gentiles had to conform to their standards to maintain fellowship. Inflexibility builds walls, not bridges.

A Church Ethnically Divided

The leadership structure of the Jerusalem church has been addressed already. But we will consider it further to see the implications of its leadership style.

The top leaders in Jerusalem were Hebraic Jews, and there is little evidence that this changed. The only Hellenistic Jew coming into this group seems to have been Silas who, according to Acts 15, was with the leaders in Jerusalem. It is worth noting that after Silas goes to Antioch he does not return to Jerusalem but resides in Antioch and travels with Paul on his missionary journeys. Could it be that Silas was more at home with the leadership in Antioch than the leadership in Jerusalem?

> Then the apostles and elders, with the whole church, decided to choose some of their own men and send them to Antioch with Paul and Barnabas. They chose Judas (called Barsabbas) and Silas, two men who were leaders among the brothers.
>
> Acts 15:22

At the least there was a high concentration of Hebraic Jews in leadership in Jerusalem. This would naturally lead to a leadership style and worldview that would fit the Hebraic people but might marginalize the Hellenistic Jews and Gentile converts.

The development of the Hellenistic Christian community presented a challenge to the leadership at Jerusalem. They had two choices: Either they could incorporate the Hellenists into the community of faith in such a way that the latter were given freedom to express themselves in the church family, or they could allow two distinct communities to develop side by side, each with its own expression.

The Jerusalem church chose the latter approach. This decision seemed to remove several potential problems but, because it did not address these issues, it reduced the church's future effectiveness. The issues of cultural differences, if fully addressed and embraced, would have brought pressure on the leadership and might have eventually changed the core values of the church. This would have moved the Jerusalem church toward being a community that could fully embrace the mandate of mission.

With the decision to develop separately, the power structure of the church created a problem. In any situation, those who have the final authority dictate what happens and how it happens. In this case we see the development of two groups of leaders—the Hebraic leaders who were in the place of power, and the Hellenistic leaders who worked under the oversight of the Hebraic ones. Differences are inevitable under such an arrangement. The ethnic group that is under the dominant group never reaches its full potential and will eventually move away. We see this in the development of the Hellenistic church at Antioch and in the movement of the Hellenistic leaders to this location.

In 1982 in Christchurch, New Zealand, Chih Yunn and I were involved in pioneering the first Chinese church in the city. Because we were already committed to an existing church, we did not seek to start another church but to develop a Chinese service as part of this church. This led to some interesting dynamics, and we saw in a small way the issues that the church in Jerusalem must have encountered as they developed a church divided by ethnicity.

The leadership in Christchurch at that time consisted of godly men whom we greatly respected, but they were all white Anglo-Saxons (as I am), whereas the Chinese church was led by a mixture of Westerners and Chinese who did not fit into the same way of thinking as the leaders who were in charge of the church overall. Because the direction and expression of the church flowed out from the senior leaders, the cultural differences of the Chinese could not be addressed and incorporated into the ethos of the church. This led to those in the Chinese section of the church feeling marginalized, with many feeling that it would be better if they came out from under the covering of the mother church and started their own church. Because issues like this were never identified and therefore never addressed, in time the Chinese left the church and several independent Chinese churches were established in the city.

The Outcome of the Jerusalem Church

Jerusalem started well, with an outstanding move of God. However, the core values of the church, and especially of its leaders, hindered it from reaching its full potential. As someone once said, "The seeds of destruction are in the foundation," and this saying seems to apply here. The leaders were inflexible and unwilling, or unable, to move outside of their comfort zone in order to participate in what they were called to do.

Yet even in this church there were some who had the ability to move the church forward. It is interesting to note that, although the monocultural mindset of the church limited its expression, God still took these people and used them within the life of the church at Jerusalem. Then He used those who were willing to go and build a new church in Antioch with a different worldview.

As the church in Antioch developed, the focus of attention moved away from Jerusalem. One of the last things mentioned about Jerusalem was its need for financial help from all the other churches because of famine.

During this time some prophets came down from Jerusalem to Antioch. One of them, named Agabus, stood up and through the Spirit predicted that a severe famine would spread over the entire Roman world. (This happened during the reign of Claudius.) The disciples, each according to his ability, decided to provide help for the brothers living in Judea. This they did, sending their gift to the elders by Barnabas and Saul.

Acts 11:27–30

The famine was evidently widespread yet, interestingly, offerings were collected from all the churches in the Roman Empire to help one church only—the Jerusalem church. Having started out rich in resources, the Jerusalem church seems to have changed to the point where it was dependent on outside daughter churches for its very survival. Does this suggest the church was no longer moving forward, full of vision and impact? Sadly, it seems to have lost its resources, its community and its way.

Antioch—the Church with a Kingdom Mentality

Antioch was a Syrian city built by Antiochus Seleucus, a general who served under Alexander the Great and assumed command after his death. It became the seat of authority for the Syrian kings of the Macedonian race, and later for the Roman governors of the eastern provinces. At the time the church was planted in Antioch it was one of the most celebrated cities of the east. It was the third most important city in the whole Roman Empire, Rome and Alexandria alone being more important.

The geographical situation made Antioch an ideal trading center. Its harbor of Seleucia provided a haven to all the ships of the Mediterranean, and the city was readily accessible by caravans from Mesopotamia and Arabia. This resulted in Antioch, a city of half a million, having a wide cultural mix, including Syrians, Romans, Greeks, Arabs, Persians, Armenians, Parthians, Cappadocians and Jews. One-seventh of Antioch's population was Jewish.

Core Values of the Antioch Church

The core values of the leaders of the Antioch church are not easy to discern, as little is given to us of their backgrounds, apart from Paul's. We can, however, extrapolate some of the core values of the *church* from what we have read about it. We will focus here on those core values that particularly impacted the church at Antioch as they pertained to mission.

The Background of the Antioch Church

The church at Antioch was birthed out of a people movement. Because the apostles were either unable or unwilling to go, they sent instead a Hellenistic Jew named Barnabas. Thus Hellenistic leadership molded the expression and direction of this church.

Now those who had been scattered by the persecution in connection with Stephen traveled as far as Phoenicia, Cyprus and Antioch, telling the message only to Jews. Some of them, however, men from Cyprus and Cyrene, went to Antioch and began to speak to Greeks also, telling them the good news about the Lord Jesus. The Lord's hand was with them, and a great number of people believed and turned to the Lord.

News of this reached the ears of the church at Jerusalem, and they sent Barnabas to Antioch. When he arrived and saw the evidence of the grace of God, he was glad and encouraged them all to remain true to the Lord with all their hearts. He was a good man, full of the Holy Spirit and faith, and a great number of people were brought to the Lord.

Then Barnabas went to Tarsus to look for Saul, and when he found him, he brought him to Antioch. So for a whole year Barnabas and Saul met with the church and taught great numbers of people. The disciples were called Christians first at Antioch.

Acts 11:19–26

When we look at who rose to the top level of leadership in the church at Antioch, we see significant differences from the leadership of the church at Jerusalem.

In the church at Antioch there were prophets and teachers: Barnabas, Simeon called Niger, Lucius of Cyrene, Manaen (who had been brought up with Herod the tetrarch) and Saul. While they were worshiping the Lord and fasting, the Holy Spirit said, "Set apart for me Barnabas and Saul for the work to which I have called them." So after they had fasted and prayed, they placed their hands on them and sent them off.

Acts 13:1–3

Scripture specifically identifies the significant leaders at Antioch, and as we look at these people we can glean a little of their backgrounds.

Barnabas. A Hellenistic Jew from Cyprus whose original name was Joseph, Barnabas was from the tribe of Levi. He had spent much time in Jerusalem, where he was converted, and was later sent to Antioch where he assumed a position of leadership.

Simeon Niger. "Niger" is a Latin name meaning "black." Nothing more is known of him than is mentioned here, but it would seem likely that his skin color was dark and that he was of non-Jewish background.

Lucius of Cyrene. Cyrene was a North African port, and Lucius's name indicates Greek roots. So he was either a Greek or a Hellenistic Jew and is mentioned as being with Paul when Paul wrote his letter to the Romans.

Manaen. This man had been brought up with Herod Antipas, the tetrarch of Galilee and a descendant of the Edomites. The Greek word translated "brought up" denotes one who was educated or nourished along with another. From this fact, and the origin of his name, it would be logical to conclude he was connected with the royal family. He was, therefore, highly likely to be an Edomite of rank and education.

Paul. A Hellenistic Jew from Tarsus whose original name was Saul, he was from the tribe of Benjamin and had spent much time in Jerusalem. He was converted on the road to Damascus, spent three years in Arabia, returned to Jerusalem, and was sent from there to Tarsus, where he stayed until Barnabas brought him to Antioch.

From this overview we can see that the leadership in Antioch was anything but monocultural. At the top level there was a core value of embracing the nations. It was a genuinely inclusive church, allowing everyone to have ownership of the vision, and people were not marginalized as they were in Jerusalem.

The leadership displayed a visionary attitude in initiating a time to seek God to find out what He was calling them to do. Rather than responding to a need that had come to their attention, they intentionally responded to the mandate God had given them. This visionary leadership understood the times and seasons and had faith to build for the future.

A Focus on Harvest

Unlike the church at Jerusalem, the leaders of the Antioch church were not Hebraic Jews but predominantly Hellenists. It was at Jerusalem that the "Kingdom restoration" theology of Jesus returning to reign in a natural kingdom held greatest influence. It would not have been easy for Antioch to express this value. If it had been a core value in Antioch there would have been a stronger linkage with Jerusalem, and Jewish values would have been more influential in the direction of the church. The fact that the leadership in Antioch strongly resisted this influence lends weight to the argument that Antioch did not buy into this "Kingdom restoration" mentality.

The focus on the harvest is seen clearly in two ways. First, when Barnabas saw the need in Antioch he did not return to Jerusalem for help, which might have been the logical thing to do. Instead he looked to Paul. This reveals something of Barnabas's values. It was not just mature leadership that Barnabas saw as important, but leadership that understood what was happening in Antioch and knew how to gather the harvest. Second, it was in Antioch that the first intentional mission occurred. This was not so much responding to what God was doing, but intentionally going where nothing was happening and "making" it happen.

The values that made the church at Antioch what it was are expressed in the writings of Paul. Paul had a great influence in the development of the Antioch church. Paul's passion was to go where the Gospel had not been preached and build the Kingdom of God. His heart's desire was to live in such a way that he could reach people from the widest range of backgrounds and circumstances. This demonstrated the fact that the church then had a core value of focusing on the harvest.

A Church That Was Flexible

Antioch differed from Jerusalem in its multicultural mindset. Several factors influenced this. First, its early leaders were Hellenistic Jews who were comfortable operating cross-culturally. Second, it was in Antioch that a large number of Greeks became Christians. This would have moved the church from being predominantly Jewish to being a community that was, at the least, so mixed that the people would have needed to address multicultural issues. Third,

Antioch was a large multicultural city, and those who grew up in it were exposed to a variety of cultural influences. This forced the church to address the issue of reaching the nations in the city, laying the foundation for reaching the nations in the Empire.

Also, a core value of life and death seemed to characterize the Antioch church. When one is dealing with people from a pagan background, they come into the community of faith with all their messed-up lives. It takes time for issues to be dealt with, and sometimes things are not clearly resolved until the next generation. This is seen in the difference between the teachings of Jesus and the teachings of Paul regarding marriage. Paul seems to have been more tolerant than Jesus, but they were talking to different audiences. Jesus was talking to the Jewish community, which in this case can be likened to a Christian community that has been under the influence of the Gospel for several generations. Paul wrote to a Christian community that had recently come out of paganism. These people had messed-up lives—many were married but had mistresses as well. In addition, temple prostitution was a way of life. Paul's response was not to judge them but to encourage them to sort out their lives.

When it came to leadership, Paul insisted on monogamous marriage. The leader was to model the Christian lifestyle. In this way the standard was set for the church and, as the church matured, the standards of the leaders would influence it.

It is interesting to note, however, that Paul never once spoke against polygamy. This was not because he agreed with it but because life and death were more important than right and wrong. We also observe that the common factors in all the churches Paul wrote to were heresy and immorality. Paul's motivation was to bring life rather than to lay down the law, but in doing so he clearly presented the truth and God's standards.

A Church Ethnically United

When some Jewish Christians from Jerusalem came to the church at Antioch, they had a problem with the Greek Christians.

> Some men came down from Judea to Antioch and were teaching the brothers: "Unless you are circumcised, according to the custom taught by Moses, you cannot be saved." This brought Paul and Barnabas into sharp dispute and debate with them. So Paul and Barnabas were appointed, along with some other believers, to go up to Jerusalem to see the apostles and elders about this question.
>
> Acts 15:1–2

This suggests that the visitors did not connect only with the Jewish Christians in Antioch, but with a community that at least contained Greek Christians. The implication is that Antioch did not separate people according to their ethnicity. This is further illustrated in an incident documented in Paul's letter to the Galatians. In this narrative Peter has arrived and is fellowshipping with the Christians, both Greeks and Jews. Later, some followers of James, the brother of Jesus, came from Jerusalem. When they arrived, Peter withdrew from fellowshipping with the Gentile Christians and fellowshipped only with Jewish ones. Even Barnabas was drawn into the same behavior. But when the situation came to the notice of Paul he confronted them about their wrongdoing.

> When Peter came to Antioch, I opposed him to his face, because he was clearly in the wrong. Before certain men came from James, he used to eat with the Gentiles. But when they arrived, he began to draw back and separate himself from the Gentiles because he was afraid of those who belonged to the circumcision group. The other Jews joined him in

his hypocrisy, so that by their hypocrisy even Barnabas was led astray.

When I saw that they were not acting in line with the truth of the gospel, I said to Peter in front of them all, "You are a Jew, yet you live like a Gentile and not like a Jew. How is it, then, that you force Gentiles to follow Jewish customs?"

Galatians 2:11–14

One fact stands out clearly: The church was not divided along ethnic lines; if it had been, this whole conflict would never have happened.

Evidently in Antioch the interaction between different people groups was far stronger than in Jerusalem. Dividing people according to their customs and ways of doing things was just not done. It was not that Paul was against the Jewish traditions (for example, he circumcised Timothy and took part in Old Testament customs of purification), but he was against imposing unnecessary regulations on the Christians that had no significance to them and could have ruptured the fellowship. Also, the leadership in Antioch was clear about what it wanted and where it was going. To them, this was an issue worth standing up for.

[Paul] came to Derbe and then to Lystra, where a disciple named Timothy lived, whose mother was a Jewess and a believer, but whose father was a Greek. The brothers at Lystra and Iconium spoke well of him. Paul wanted to take him along on the journey, so he circumcised him because of the Jews who lived in that area, for they all knew that his father was a Greek.

Acts 16:1–3

Paul greeted them and reported in detail what God had done among the Gentiles through his ministry.

When they heard this, they praised God. Then they said to Paul: "You see, brother, how many thousands of Jews have believed, and all of them are zealous for the law. They have

81

been informed that you teach all the Jews who live among the Gentiles to turn away from Moses, telling them not to circumcise their children or live according to our customs. What shall we do? They will certainly hear that you have come, so do what we tell you. There are four men with us who have made a vow. Take these men, join in their purification rites and pay their expenses, so that they can have their heads shaved. Then everybody will know there is no truth in these reports about you, but that you yourself are living in obedience to the law. As for the Gentile believers, we have written to them our decision that they should abstain from food sacrificed to idols, from blood, from the meat of strangled animals and from sexual immorality."

The next day Paul took the men and purified himself along with them. Then he went to the temple to give notice of the date when the days of purification would end and the offering would be made for each of them.

Acts 21:19–26

The Outcome of the Antioch Church

The core values of the church at Antioch allowed it to become capable of fulfilling the Great Commission. This multicultural church did not allow people to settle into their comfort zones; rather, it created an environment where the *ethne* of the world and the church collided. The mandate of Jesus was not something that needed to be imposed on this church—it was part of its fabric, the reason for its very existence. It produced people with cultural awareness, where bicultural people felt accepted and able to play a part. In Antioch, a church was birthed that had the vision and ability to extend a mission thrust from its local area to the whole of the Roman Empire.

In summary, then, what created the difference between the church in Jerusalem and the church in Antioch?

First, the expression and direction of a church is molded by its leadership. Jerusalem's leadership was predominantly monocultural Hebraic Jews while Antioch's leadership was multicultural with a strong Hellenistic influence.

Second, the core values of both churches were different. Both churches understood that Jesus was to reign over the nations. However, the focus of the two churches in this respect was different. Jerusalem's focus was on the return to rulership, with Jerusalem being the obvious and biblical location for the seat of His reign. Antioch focused on the ingathering of the nations, and so its focus was on "the harvest." Antioch was multicultural in flavor, and under these conditions the bicultural people were able to develop and impact the Greco-Roman world. If the bicultural person was the key ingredient in effectively crossing the cultural barrier, then how can we identify those who have this ability?

six

The Bicultural Person

As we look at the whole concept of mission as outlined in the book of Acts, we see the major role bicultural people play in its accomplishment. So the question arises: How do we determine who is bicultural? In the Western world we tend to see education as the answer to our problems, and today we have courses that teach missions with the aim of bringing mission awareness to the church. Many people believe that by taking these courses and then going on a short-term mission trip they have become cross-cultural. I myself have worked in cross-cultural and multicultural situations for more than thirty years, and yet I would not consider myself to be bicultural in the scriptural sense. The problem is that we have not set any criteria by which the term *cross-cultural* can be defined. It becomes an arbitrary assessment, usually made by someone who wants to be a missionary or an organization that is placing missionaries on the field.

One way to define biculturalism is to identify the person in Scripture who best fits this description and draw from his life those things that qualify him to be bicultural. From this we can build a model that can be used as a standard for identifying people with bicultural abilities. The person who I consider best fits the profile is the apostle Paul. However, before we look at his life, we first need to define some terms—monocultural, multicultural, cross-cultural and bicultural—to provide a clear understanding of what we are talking about.

A *monocultural* situation is where only one culture is evident or one culture dominates in its expression. Up until this century most people have been monocultural. However, changes are occurring because of the global movement of people and with all major cities becoming multicultural.

A *multicultural* situation is where many cultures exist in one location and have the opportunity to add to the overall expression of the community. I doubt if one person can be multicultural, but it is possible to live in a multicultural situation. This is the environment of the 21st century.

A *cross-cultural* person is someone who can traverse from one culture to another. That is, they are comfortable in either culture, not just in terms of enjoying the food and customs but also in being able to understand and operate within the worldview of either group.

A *bicultural* person is one who lives within two cultures; his world is two worlds, each with a different worldview, core values, beliefs and customs. A bicultural person is completely cross-cultural and moves between the cultures as if they were one.

A Man Named Paul

We are able to glean some understanding of biculturalism from Paul's life. First, he was one of the key men whom God used, and second, we know more about his background than that of any other bicultural person of his day. This makes him a logical role model.

When they heard him speak to them in Aramaic, they became very quiet. Then Paul said: "I am a Jew, born in Tarsus of Cilicia, but brought up in this city. Under Gamaliel I was thoroughly trained in the law of our fathers and was just as zealous for God as any of you are today."

Acts 22:2–3

If anyone else thinks he has reasons to put confidence in the flesh, I have more: circumcised on the eighth day, of the people of Israel, of the tribe of Benjamin, a Hebrew of Hebrews; in regard to the law, a Pharisee; as for zeal, persecuting the church; as for legalistic righteousness, faultless.

Philippians 3:4–6

For you have heard of my previous way of life in Judaism, how intensely I persecuted the church of God and tried to destroy it. I was advancing in Judaism beyond many Jews of my own age and was extremely zealous for the traditions of my fathers. But when God, who set me apart from birth and called me by his grace, was pleased to reveal his Son in me so that I might preach him among the Gentiles, I did not consult any man, nor did I go up to Jerusalem to see those who were apostles before I was, but I went immediately into Arabia and later returned to Damascus.

Then after three years, I went up to Jerusalem to get acquainted with Peter and stayed with him fifteen days. I saw none of the other apostles—only James, the Lord's brother. I assure you before God that what I am writing you is no lie. Later I went to Syria and Cilicia. I was personally unknown to the churches of Judea that are in Christ. They only heard the report: "The man who formerly persecuted us is now preaching the faith he once tried to destroy." And they praised God because of me.

Galatians 1:13–24

These three passages give us insights into Paul's background and allow us to identify some of the key things that made him bicultural.

Paul was born in Tarsus. This was the capital city of Cilicia, found on the banks of the Cydnus River in the province of Asia Minor. It was a Grecian commercial center and a city of great learning. In Paul's day it was the site of one of the three top universities of the Roman Empire, thought by some to be more prominent than Athens or Alexandria. What we do know is that the university at Tarsus furnished tutors to the imperial family. Paul once referred to the status of Tarsus when he called it "no ordinary city" (Acts 21:39).

We can assume that, although Paul later moved to Palestine, he had lived long enough in Tarsus to pick up the worldview of the Greco-Roman culture. If we consider how our own worldview is developed, we will realize that most of our values and cultural perceptions are developed at a young age. This would mean that Paul was Hellenized as a young man before he reached Jerusalem.

Paul moved to Jerusalem, where he learned the local language, Aramaic. Here he was educated by Gamaliel, reputed to be the top rabbinical teacher of his day. In those days a boy would be in his teens when he entered the rabbinical school. His training was thoroughly Jewish, rooted and grounded in the Scriptures of the Old Covenant and the traditions of the elders as recorded in the Talmud. Paul's command of biblical truth is displayed in his writings and communication with Jewish converts. He quotes from the Pentateuch, the Prophets and the Psalms, literally and freely. He shows he is a master of the hidden depths of the Word of God and is able to throw light on obscure passages.

Paul's life and study in Jerusalem caused him to become quite skilled in Jewish thought and tradition, and he fully embraced the worldview of the Jewish people. The process did not start when he went to Jerusalem, however, but would have been built into him from his earliest years. Paul had been part of the Jewish community in Tarsus that built its life around the local synagogue. Here he would have learned the values and traditions of his people and the Scriptures known today as the Old Testament; here his identity as a Jewish man would have been grounded. His passion for this Jewish identity can be seen in his great zeal to keep the traditions of his people pure. We see this in his persecution of the new sect who were later to be called Christians. Paul's boasting of his lineage, being of the tribe of Benjamin, shows he fully identified with his Jewish roots.

He lived in Jerusalem until after his conversion. After that, during the subsequent unrest, the apostles sent him back to Tarsus, where he remained for the next ten years. He is likely to have had friends or relatives there. In those days relocation and travel were not as common or convenient as they are today, and for general living you needed help from your community to survive. So Paul's relocation to Tarsus indicates a high degree of connectedness to it. There is no indication a church had been established there at the time, so Paul was not able to use the church as a base to help his relocation.

From the time of his conversion, Paul was aware of his call to the Gentiles. It is logical to conclude that during these ten years in Tarsus he returned to his Greco-Roman roots as he prepared himself for the mission of his life. Also, under Gamaliel, Paul spent half of his time learning the Greek language, philosophy and rhetoric. This was because Gamaliel's vision was to prepare his students for the missionizing of the nations. Paul was therefore well acquainted with Greek culture and philosophy and literature. This is seen in the didactic style of his letters and in his allusions to other religions and philosophies. His occasional quotations from Greek poets reveal his understanding of the Greco-Roman worldview.

At this point he changed his name. Formerly he was called Saul, a Hebrew name, but now he was called Paul, a non-Jewish name. This in itself suggests an acceptance of his Greco-Roman roots. We know Paul was able to read and write in Greek as some of his letters were written by his own hand rather than by an amanuensis (secretary). Since the people he was writing to did not speak Aramaic, we can infer that the originals were written in Greek, the common language.

Paul embraced both cultures and took from each of them whatever was helpful. He did not hesitate to announce his Roman citizenship when it suited him to do so, but he also used his Jewish roots to advantage. One of his core values is expressed in 1 Corinthians 9:22 when he said, "I have become all things to all men so that by all possible means I might save some."

From this brief look at Paul's roots we glean four important facts about his bicultural qualifications:

- He was born and raised in a minority community, interrelating with a group considered to be the host community.
- Paul spent many years in both cultures, to such an extent that he was equally at home in each.
- This preparation was not something God did in Paul's life after selecting him for mission work. The Lord prepared him from the day he was born. In fact, this preparation was the prerequisite for becoming a missionary, not an optional extra.
- Paul was equally at home in, and equally valued, both cultures.

Because Paul was bicultural, he could see what God was doing in the Jewish world and could extract the essence of the Gospel and transfer it into the Greco-Roman world without attaching Jewish cultural trappings. It is important today that we identify bicultural people and release them into their calling.

Who can identify who is bicultural? People who have a proven bicultural or cross-cultural ability are the ones who can identify others with the same ability.

There are prepared bicultural people today who will be effective in taking the Gospel across the cultural barrier to plant God's grace in the fertile soil of their communities. In 1989 I first met Uong Nguyen. Uong was a refugee from North Vietnam. He had been a soldier fighting against the Khmer Rouge in Cambodia. He was captured by Khmer soldiers and held on the border of Cambodia and Thailand. Eventually, Uong was released by the intervention of the International Red Cross. From captivity among the Khmer Rouge he was sent to a Thai prison and then on to a refugee camp.

Five years later, he arrived in Australia knowing no one, a young man alone in a strange world. It was through divine providence that Uong became connected to the church and surrendered his life to Jesus. This started a remarkable chapter in his life. Before coming to Australia he had no intention or desire to leave his country or people and settle in a foreign land. I have watched over the last seventeen years of this man's journey. Not only have I seen him grow in his faith, but I have also watched him grow in his ability to live in a Western community. Today, Uong is married to Lyn, a New Zealander, and they have two children, Tan Viet and Linh Nhat. He is well established in Australia and calls Australia home. Yet, despite all of this, he has never lost his connection to his own family in Vietnam or his passion to reach out to Vietnamese wherever they may be.

Today, Uong heads up the pastoral care team in our church and is effective in ministering to all people regardless of their ethnic background. In 1999 I traveled with Uong to Vietnam and there met his family, which consists of several hundred people. Up until that time I had not been aware of the opportunity that had opened to us when Uong became part of our church family. All I understood was that Uong was the son of a villager from the Red River Delta in North Vietnam. Yet when I visited this family, I was introduced to high-ranking army officers, Confucius scholars, Taoist mediums, university lecturers, politicians and lawyers. It is into this family of influence that Uong has been able to bring the Gospel without the trappings of Western culture. This is due to the fact that Uong has grown up in two worlds. Because of his unique background, he is able to take the Gospel that he has experienced in his Australian world and present it without its cultural trappings into his Vietnamese world.

The Environment under Which Bicultural People Best Develop

When we look at the churches in our cities we see a common process occurring. A misconception prevalent in the Christian community is that churches grow best in homogeneous units, therefore monocultural churches must be the will of God. Because of this, we have tended to develop monocultured churches without asking any serious questions. When we discover a sizable number of people of a particular ethnic group, we focus on planting a church among them. Also, when people from a new ethnic group come into our midst, their leaders rarely find a place of expression in our established monocultural churches. Those with leadership ability who do come into our churches are actively encouraged to gather their own people, set up a service to cater to them and build a new ethnic congregation.

This process can happen in various ways. A daughter church may be developed that uses the same facilities, a completely autonomous church may be set up with its own facilities or the ethnic group may remain part of the initiating church but as a semi-autonomous congregation. Regardless of which structure is adopted, the result will be the same: The people with the leadership potential and cultural exposure that allow them to become effective bicultural missionaries will be denied the opportunity to develop this skill. By encouraging them to remain primarily within their own culture and to use their leadership skills only among their own people, we close the door to all but the few who have the tenacity to break out of the box we place them in. This preoccupation with building ethnic churches and congregations has markedly reduced the availability of bicultural people within our churches.

In places where churches have decided not to reach immigrants by building ethnic churches, their approach has been to encourage the immigrant to become part of the existing church. However, in most cases, the issue of the church's culture is not addressed. In Australia these churches are usually white, Anglo-Saxon and middle-class, having their own ethnic cultural values and worldview. Because these values have arisen historically, they have been accepted without question, and it is therefore unusual for members to reevaluate themselves. Those in positions of influence tend to maintain the current values of the church and are usually not prepared to move out of their comfort zones. They expect immigrants to embrace the existing church culture and to learn "how we do things here." This approach may result in one of two outcomes.

First, the immigrants may feel marginalized, and although they continue to attend, they may not become fully part of the church. There is always a gap. Consequently, they may eventually move on to another church or, if there are sufficient numbers, they may well start their own ethnic fellowship. Alternatively, those who fully integrate may do so at the cost of losing their own ethnic identity. Thus they lose the opportunity to develop bicultural awareness and, although they may become valued members of the congregation and be held up as examples of immigrants who have become successful in this country, their potential as bicultural servants is lost.

At Antioch a high value was placed on building a church that embraced many ethnic groups, and its leaders came from a variety of cultural backgrounds. This was in contrast to the Jerusalem church, which developed along separate ethnic lines and whose leadership team comprised only one ethnic group. When we look at the end result of these two churches, we see that Antioch attracted and developed far more bicultural people than did Jerusalem. Thus, Antioch was far more effective in spreading the Gospel, both geographically and culturally.

As we look at these two churches in Acts, we see the church that best developed and attracted bicultural people was the one that had multiethnic leadership. This resulted in a church that was not tied to any ethnic worldview. It also promoted the mingling of ethnic communities instead of allowing people to live within their comfort zones. Antioch models what I consider to be the expression of a multicultural church.

The multicultural church has the greatest ability to develop bicultural people, as this environment does not allow people to remain isolated in their own comfort zones. Rather, it challenges prejudices and monocultural values. As the church develops values that allow it to be multicultural, it will be able to identify bicultural people and develop their potential to effectively move the Gospel across cultural barriers.

Paul exemplifies the bicultural person in his ability to function effectively in two worlds. But are there other issues that need to be investigated so that we can be effective in reaching the nations?

seven

The Incarnate Principle of Mission

When we come to look at the attitudes and values a missionary should have, we need look no further than Jesus himself.

Your attitude should be the same as that of Christ Jesus:

Who, being in very nature God,
did not consider equality with God something to
be grasped,
but made himself nothing,
taking the very nature of a servant,
being made in human likeness.
And being found in appearance as a man,
he humbled himself
and became obedient to death—
even death on a cross!

Philippians 2:5–8

Principle one: He left behind everything of His previous culture. Jesus did not bring any of the privileges of His heavenly culture when He entered the Jewish one.

95

Principle two: He limited His resources to what was available to all in that culture. Jesus deliberately limited Himself to the resources and understanding of the Jewish culture so that the Jews could understand and accept the revelation of God.

Principle three: He was committed for His whole life. Jesus did not come for a short-term assignment. The commitment was for the rest of His life, and He died in the fulfillment of His calling.

Because mission has been shaped by the Western world, there are several concepts influencing our understanding of it that I suggest are not entirely biblical. In general, the Church has failed to make the hard calls when it comes to setting the expectations and requirements for missionaries, primarily because, as pastors, we would find it difficult to follow these principles ourselves if we were called by God to go to another ethnic group.

First, we have an individualistic view of the calling of God. We believe we are called, but that our children may not necessarily be. But when we look at Abraham, we see that God called him and his whole family, including all his servants. Abraham's calling was intergenerational. A fundamental principle of Scripture is that God places us in families and deals with us as families. If God calls us to go, then all who belong to our family become involved in that call.

Second, we want our children to have the best opportunities, and we do not want our obedience to the call of God to affect those who were not part of the decision making. Therefore, we may feel obligated to send our children to special schools that maintain the standards of the schools back home, or alternatively, send them home to be educated, as the situation in which we find ourselves does not give them the opportunities we feel they need.

Career missionaries have had to make hard—even agonizing—decisions over the years, and God knows their hearts, but we need to think about the incarnate principle

Jesus modeled. Will our choices identify us as outsiders who have come to help but who are not really "one" with those to whom we present the Gospel? Will our actions cause us to lose credibility if, by them, we imply that God is not able to meet all our needs in this new environment? Do we present to them a God who is not worth following wholeheartedly?

If we are not ready to make some hard decisions, we need to ask whether we are really called or prepared to pay the price of that call. The argument that we should not deprive our children of their right to the educational opportunities we enjoyed may reveal our individualistic Western approach. The fundamental question is this: Did God call us as a family or as an individual, and are we called for life, or are we going back?

In our missions today, we tend to send potted plants rather than transplants. When a gardener puts a plant in a pot he takes the soil that is best for the plant being potted. The plant will take root and flourish to a degree, but it will never reach its full potential. A transplant is taken out of the soil where it germinated and taken to a new location where it is placed in the soil of that location. Here it has to adjust to the new conditions to take root and grow. Once it is established, however, it is difficult to relocate without seriously damaging the plant.

I remember while in New Zealand we used to grow an indoor potted plant called a rubber tree. This was an ornamental tree, not the rubber tree that produced latex. We had one in our lounge, and I enjoyed viewing this glossy-leafed plant. It wasn't until I came to Sydney that I saw this tree planted in the soil. It was nothing like the potted version that I knew; rather it was a huge tree that grew to over 66 feet high and over 50 feet wide. It was a completely different plant. When, as missionaries, we go to a new location, are we, for the sake of our children, building a little bit of home for their future, or are we taking root in the soil of the new location?

I believe in the "Ruth" principle: We are called forward into a new community and are asked to identify totally with that community. We are never called back, although we may be called forward to a new community, or even called forward to the community we came from. If we have the attitude that, when the job is done, we will go back, we will never fully belong to the community to which we are called.

> "Look," said Naomi, "your sister-in-law is going back to her people and her gods. Go back with her."
>
> But Ruth replied, "Don't urge me to leave you or to turn back from you. Where you go I will go, and where you stay I will stay. Your people will be my people and your God my God. Where you die I will die, and there I will be buried. May the LORD deal with me, be it ever so severely, if anything but death separates you and me." When Naomi realized that Ruth was determined to go with her, she stopped urging her.
>
> Ruth 1:15–18

Today we place many activities under the umbrella of "missions." This can make it difficult for a sending church to identify those who are, in fact, missionaries. The term "short-term mission team" suggests that a brief ministry trip to another country makes the participant a missionary. There are people who go to another country to be involved in a specific task, usually skills-based, to assist the church in that location. They may be considered missionaries, too. But these activities rarely come to grips with the issue of incarnation, which is fundamental to the process of planting the Gospel within a new ethnic group.

Around 1986, Dennis and Kathy Balcombe, missionaries in Hong Kong, came to Christchurch, New Zealand, to be the guest speakers at our Chinese church. It was during this time that we came to know Dennis and Kathy and were able to see this incarnate principle working in the lives of this American-born couple. As Dennis ministered in Cantonese to the Chinese in Christchurch, it was amazing to see the response of those he ministered to. Without exception the Chinese would come and say to us that they could not believe that a European could speak their language so well; in fact, many recognized that he was a better speaker than they were, in his pronunciation, tonal expression and depth of language. They said he was more Chinese than they were. My wife, Chih Yunn, who comes from Hong Kong and Malaysia, testifies to the Balcombes' ability and commitment to embrace fully the people they felt called to give their lives to.

As the Balcombes were staying in our home we witnessed how committed they were to embracing their adopted people. While they were staying with us their daughter back in Hong Kong was having her birthday, and so Kathy called back to talk to her. It was to our surprise that when Kathy was talking to her daughter, both of them spoke Cantonese, not English. Even though this was a simple thing, we were struck by the level of commitment that this family had embraced as they were transplanted from their American homeland into Chinese soil. This family has made a significant contribution to the church of China, and I doubt if the extent of their far-reaching influence will ever be fully known. Yet I am convinced that the degree of impact that they have experienced is built on the foundation of their incarnational lifestyle.

Jesus, as the greatest missionary, totally identified with the Jewish culture. He did not have a short-term mentality but was committed for life. We, likewise, should have the same attitude. As we look into this subject, it would not be hard to form a view that cross-cultural mission is for a select few who are specially equipped. Does this mean that the rest of us do not need to be involved in the task of reaching the nations? We will consider this question in the next chapter.

eight

The Mandate Is for All

A common challenge faced by those involved in missionary organizations is that of mobilizing the Church to mission. Matthew 28:19 is often quoted: "Go and make disciples of all nations, baptizing them in the name of the Father and of the Son and of the Holy Spirit."

Those with a focus on missions rightly say it is the will of God for us to go. We do not need a word from God to go, we need a word from God to stay, because the Scripture is God's revealed will and tells us to go. However, we know it is not practical for everyone to go. If all went, who would support them? So we modify this concept by saying there are many different ways of being involved in the going. We can pray, we can give, and we can be part of the home support team of those who are on the field. This, we say, is all part of the going.

If we look at Matthew 28:19 closely, we realize this interpretation hinges on our concept of the word "nations." Without thinking, we interpret this as a geographical location, so that to "go" means to travel from where we are now to another place. Yet we have already seen that the word *nations* is better translated as "ethnic group." Looked at from this perspective, the Scripture takes on new meaning. It is not telling us that we have to "move" geographically; rather we must "go" culturally. This might or might not mean a geographical relocation, but it does mean God intends everyone to move out of his or her ethnic group. We are all to move out of our comfort zone to embrace another ethnic group in such a way that we make disciples from among them.

As a pastor, I am told that my job is to make disciples. In fact the issue of the Great Commission is not about getting decisions but about making disciples. I must admit that I have struggled with the whole concept of making disciples as it has so often been associated with a study course that will help in making wonderful disciples. As I look back on my own experience of being discipled, I realize that no one "discipled" me; I just grew up in the church and became a disciple. Therefore, I find it difficult to know how to "disciple" others.

It is interesting to listen to comments from ministers who come to speak at our church. One of the oft-repeated comments is, "You have so many quality people in this church." When you consider this comment against the fact that most of these people are first-generation Christians with no Christian heritage, usually coming from Buddhism, Hinduism, Islam or atheism, you have to ask the question, How did this happen? Why, without any formal discipleship program, were we able to produce so many quality disciples?

As I looked at this question I had to come to the conclusion that our process of disciple making flowed out of our understanding of what church is. For those of us who come from a Western worldview, we unconsciously see church as an institution. We claim by our words that church is a family, but as I look at our actions and values, I have come to the conclusion that church, to us, is primarily the institution that is identified by the activities that are under its oversight. For the last thirty years of my life, I have worked in a non-Western world environment, and I have started to see the world through non-Western eyes. One of the differences that has been significant to me is to realize that the Eastern world in general does not see the church as an institution, unless they have been "discipled" by Western-minded people. Rather, they see the church as a family that functions with family values, not institutional values. This difference has a profound effect on the process of discipleship.

We all grow up in families, and sociologists say that 80 percent of a person's values are learned before he or she goes to school. How are these values learned? Parents do not sit down with their five-year-old children and instruct them in the values of the family so that they learn the "family values." Rather, as children live in families, they naturally pick up the values of that family. All members of the family contribute to the formation of the values of the children who are part of that family. We can identify this process as being a relational discipleship process.

I remember one time as a young married couple, Chih Yunn and I traveled to Queenstown in Otago, a province in New Zealand, for a holiday. On Sunday we visited the local New Life Church for their morning service. After the service, the pastor came up to me and greeted me with the words, "You are from Peter Morrow's church." I was surprised at this statement and asked him how he knew. His response was, "You have Peter Morrow written all over you." What was he saying? Simply that because of my relationship in the church family in Christchurch I had picked up the values of the father in that family, and that was visible to those who came in contact with me. This is the process of relational discipleship.

Church as an institution relies heavily on teaching as its method of addressing issues and solving problems. This is very noticeable in the Western church, which responds to a need by producing a study course or teaching program. We believe that change comes through enlightenment, and enlightenment comes through right understanding. But if it is true that we learn 80 percent of our values through a relational discipleship process, then we learn only 20 percent of our values through a teaching discipleship process. This means that our institutional model of training is at best inefficient in impacting lives as it does not have the ability to operate in the family relational environment.

Further, the process of discipleship in an institutional model becomes the domain of the teacher; those who do not have the ability to teach cannot easily participate in the discipleship process. The church as an institution sets the program for discipleship, and instead of all disciples making disciples we have a select few discipling the new converts. So the church does make disciples according to Christ's command in Matthew 28:19, but in our Western churches disciples are not making disciples. Instead, teachers alone are making disciples since our focus is on a teaching process.

In Matthew 12 Jesus stated who His family was. This was not a statement of rejection of His natural family but a declaration of the type of relationship that He had with His disciples. As the disciple maker, Jesus identified a value that created disciples:

> While Jesus was still talking to the crowd, his mother and brothers stood outside, wanting to speak to him. Someone told him, "Your mother and brothers are standing outside, wanting to speak to you."
>
> He replied to him, "Who is my mother, and who are my brothers?" Pointing to his disciples, he said, "Here are my mother and my brothers. For whoever does the will of my Father in heaven is my brother and sister and mother."
>
> verses 46–50

As Jesus identified this family relational environment that was operating in this first church community consisting of Jesus, His disciples and the crowd that followed Him, He clearly defines a family relationship, not with the crowd, but

104

with His disciples. I would have to conclude that the first church was built on a family relational platform, not an institutional platform. As we started a church in Cabramatta, we intentionally built on a family platform. By this I mean that church becomes a family with people seeing themselves as brothers and sisters, not just calling themselves brother and sister because they cannot remember other people's names, but members becoming uncles and aunties and fathers and mothers functioning in the life of the church.

It is in this family environment that discipleship thrives. Just as in a natural family the values are caught by the children, so also in the church that lives as a family. Discipleship ceases to be the domain of the teacher and is passed back to all disciples, who build disciples through relationship and the Word. Thus the two discipleship processes operate hand in hand, and the church as a family becomes a disciple-making community rather than a disciple-making institution.

The first church, which was Jesus and His disciples, lived out this church family relational lifestyle. Where Jesus went the disciples went, where Jesus slept they slept; they went on holidays together, they ate together and they traveled together. They did not have a special restroom for Jesus; they were family.

So when Jesus told His disciples to go and make disciples, they knew exactly what they were to do. They were to go and find others and make them a part of their family, to fully involve them in their lives and have them eat with them, travel with them, go on holiday with them and become their brothers and sisters. This was how they were discipled, and so they understood the Great Commission from this perspective. What makes this Scripture so amazing to me was that Jesus said to these monocultural Hebraic Jews—who would have nothing to do with anyone who was not Jewish— that they were to make disciples of other ethnic people. What He was saying was that to be His disciples, they must go and gather non-Jewish people and make them part of their family, giving them equal value and status, the same as they would any Jewish person.

Now let us look at our present-day situation. If the church is a family, and if discipleship is a product of the church operating as a family, the mandate of the Great Commission makes it impossible for a church to reach out only to its own kind and follow the teachings of Christ, since reaching only people like ourselves is contrary to His command in the Great Commission, which requires that I bring into my family people of different ethnos.

The building of separate ethnic churches has been encouraged, whether they are among immigrant people groups who have recently arrived here or under the auspices of congregations whose culture is that of the host nation. I suggest that this development is not scriptural. If we really wanted to obey the Great Commission, we would build multicultural churches in which cross-cultural communication would happen naturally.

The Great Commission is not something that a few select people get the opportunity to take part in. God expects every believer to be involved and has made cross-cultural discipleship available and attainable to all.

Clearly, when Jesus gave this command, His intention was that all disciples were to be reaching all the nations. None of us has a mandate to stay within the comfort zone of our own community, but we are called to step out into a bigger world than our own. Someone once said that "sacred cows make good hamburgers"! Now, we all can laugh at other people's "sacred cows," but as mission-minded people, we have our own sacred cows. Some of our "sacred cows" can be found in the way we view missions, and much of this comes from the fact that our focus is on the messenger rather than the goal.

nine

Our Emotive Response to Missions

As I have discussed this subject with others who are involved in what today we call missions, and as I have presented the understanding that missions should primarily be a function of the local church, not the mission field, and that the raising up of bicultural people for the purpose of fulfilling the Great Commission should be our major focus, I have had three responses.

But God Can Use Anyone

This is true. God can use anyone or anything. He has even used a donkey, and it is His sovereign right to use whomever He wishes. But we must not use this as an argument to ignore the principles in His Word that tell us how to transmit the Gospel into new ethnic groups. We may need to face some hard challenges in our cross-cultural endeavor, and we may need to question the programs and structures in which we have a vested interest.

What About the Hudson Taylors of This World?

Are we saying it is better to maintain a system that does not take advantage of the principles outlined in the Scriptures just because we can point to some successful people who have done great things? If our current methods have produced a handful of men and women, such as Hudson Taylor and Amy Carmichael, who have had a great impact, does it mean the model does not need to be challenged? It is not a question of success or failure but of maximizing the impact by using the best resources we have. The only way we could determine the relative effectiveness of the two models is by looking at the failure level of the current model and measuring it against the failure level of the biblical model.

In the latter we see churches planted that reflect the culture in which they take root—they are self-governing, self-supporting and self-propagating. In the whole narrative regarding church planting and those who planted them we find only one failure. That was Mark, who returned home. Why did he return home? It was not as though he was traveling in some primitive community; he was going to some of the wealthiest cities in the world where there were sizable Jewish communities. Lifestyle should not have been an issue either. The only logical explanation is that Mark's struggle was due to his monocultural Hebraic mindset; he could not function cross-culturally and so turned back. Even our best examples of mission work today cannot boast this level of success.

The question we should really be asking is this: How many Pauls and Barnabases have we missed because of the model we are currently using?

What About All Those Who Have Been Called?

This question is expressed in two ways. First, "I believe God has called me to . . ." Usually this statement is finished with the name of a country or a people. Second, it is expressed as, "God has laid on my heart . . ." Again a country or people group is mentioned.

New Life Centre Christchurch had a vision for the nations, and many people felt called to mission, far more than actually went. I remember one young man talking to me one day about the fact that he was called to China. At that time the church that he was attending had over forty Chinese students attending. They met together every Friday and had significant impact among university students. When I suggested to this young man that he should get involved with the Chinese students in the church, there was no response or interest. His call was to China as a place, not a people. Needless to say, he never once came to the Asian Group meetings or went to China as a missionary.

We need to understand the emotive content of people's perceived call. The issues revolve around "my" call and "my" destiny, which is an individualistic Western cultural response. Approaching things from this perspective makes it hard to be unbiased, but we need to remember that the primary issue is not "my" call or "my" destiny—it is that the unreached be reached! Who does the job is not too important. In the end what matters most is that within a new ethnic group a church is planted that is self-governing, self-propagating and self-supporting.

If God has given us a passion for a particular people group, we would surely want the best-equipped and best-prepared people to be given the opportunity to reach them. If we do not have the skills and heritage to accomplish the task ourselves, then we should totally support prepared persons as they are released into this mission.

Many of us from monocultural backgrounds have a heart for a specific ethnic group or groups, which is a burden that God has given to us. How we interpret this call is all-important. Currently, when we experience such a call in our hearts, we assume God wants us to be "missionaries." The reality is that many people who have this sense of call are not equipped to be effective on the overseas field, but we send them out, only to see them struggle. Some have given up after only a short time. Of those who remain, few come to the place where they are fully integrated into the culture.

So, how are we to work out the call God has placed on our lives? Are we called to lose our lives in a foreign culture, or is our role to work with those who are potentially bicultural, who are found in our community or a community where we could easily relocate to? If I were to invest in the lives of a small number of bicultural people who, in turn, went into cross-cultural situations, I believe I will have accomplished far more, with less expense, than if I had gone myself. Admittedly, this concept is not glamorous and therefore may not be popular.

In short, an emotive response to missions has damaged many lives. Certainly positive things have been accomplished in the field, but relative to the number of people sent, we cannot say it is a highly successful model. It is true that people rise to the level of their incompetence, and nowhere is this seen more clearly than in the missionary situation. Many of those who return from overseas are so hurt that they never want to be involved in a cross-cultural situation again. If these people had been encouraged to work with bicultural people in their own environment, instead of going into a situation that was beyond their competence level, we might have reduced the number of damaged people and helped others to fulfill the call on their lives.

So if we were to put aside the issue of who God uses and look at how the early Church reached the Greco-Roman world by focusing on the strategic process, what principles could we use today that would help us make missions more effective?

ten

Paul's Strategy for Church Expansion

When we look at Luke's account of the spread of the Gospel in the book of Acts, we must remember we are looking through only one window at this great event. No doubt much more happened than was recorded. At the same time, this snapshot of events was considered appropriate to become part of the canon of Scripture. While we do not claim it to be exhaustive, we do have within this account all the principles and information we need to help us get the job done. So let us look at the principles used by Paul in his task of reaching his world.

It is clear from the Scriptures that before Antioch, church planting and missions happened primarily as a response to what God was doing or as a result of persecution pressures. But at Antioch, church planting became intentional. The Hellenistic church at Antioch took seriously the mandate of Jesus to take the Gospel to the known world. Under the direction of the Holy Spirit, the church at Antioch selected what could only be described as their best leaders, and they released them for a church-planting journey, not in response to an observed need but in response to the command of God to reach all people.

There are several similarities between Paul's era and ours. Rarely in the history of the world had there been a time of comparable security that gave people freedom of movement, the ability to travel and the capacity to build and hold wealth. These factors contributed to the growth of cities of far-reaching influence, and they provided the stability under which the Gospel flourished. By stability, I do not mean an acceptance or tolerance of the Gospel message, but a strong government that enabled its citizens to live in peace. Paul encouraged Timothy to pray for those in authority so that the right conditions would prevail to enable the Gospel to be spread to all (see 1 Timothy 2:1–4).

Because the conditions of Paul's time and ours are similar, some of the principles Paul used to accomplish the task may also be relevant for us. However, we first need to understand the structure of the society in which Paul worked and how the history of colonization by the Greeks had molded the communities of Asia Minor.

The Communities of Asia Minor

At the time of Paul, Asia Minor (modern Turkey) was a meeting place of East and West. We can identify from the collection of races and societies two coexistent social systems, known as the native system and the Hellenistic system. These systems overlapped, but they corresponded in a general way to the distinction between the Greek city-state and the Asiatic village system. A deep gulf separated these two societies.

The native culture was strongest in the interior of the country and contained a large section of the population. It combined a theocratic form of government with structures resulting from a matriarchal society. The center of this community was the temple, with its many priests living off temple revenue. The common people were the servants of the gods and worked on the temple estates. The villages in which they lived were an inseparable part of the temple, and the priests were their absolute rulers. A special class performed functions in the temple service. This included, in the case of women, sometimes a service of chastity or of ceremonial prostitution. Under this structure, the whole of society was controlled by the temple life. The priests closely supervised the morals and daily routines of their people. They were their rulers, judges, helpers and healers.

The Greek city-state often started with the establishment of Greek city government in an older city with the addition of new inhabitants. These inhabitants often included Jews, whom the Greeks found to be trustworthy colonists. The goal of the rulers was the Hellenization of the country, and their example did influence the neighboring cities. The organization of the Greek and Roman cities contrasted sharply with the absolute rule of the native system. The cities enjoyed a liberal measure of self-government. Magistrates were elected, and the wealthy erected magnificent public buildings, founded schools and promoted education. The Greeks considered the Asiatic religion to be a degraded cult. This attitude caused a rift to develop between the religious life and the secular life of those who belonged to the Hellenistic system. It meant that in these communities the tight control the Asiatic religion had over the people was broken. It was into this arena that Paul went in his mission to advance the Gospel.

What Was Paul's Focus?

In Paul's journeys, we find some common factors in his mission strategy. He was led by the Holy Spirit. He did not work out a plan and then go about executing it. But, within the context of the leading of God, he operated under certain principles.

113

Paul and his companions traveled throughout the region of Phrygia and Galatia, having been kept by the Holy Spirit from preaching the word in the province of Asia. When they came to the border of Mysia, they tried to enter Bithynia, but the Spirit of Jesus would not allow them to. So they passed by Mysia and went down to Troas. During the night Paul had a vision of a man of Macedonia standing and begging him, "Come over to Macedonia and help us." After Paul had seen the vision, we got ready at once to leave for Macedonia, concluding that God had called us to preach the gospel to them.

Acts 16:6–10

Paul saw his task as more than planting churches. By targeting the Hellenistic cities rather than the Asiatic-controlled towns, he showed that he wanted to build *visionary* churches that would become launching pads for further Christian ministry to the province and beyond. He placed little emphasis on the provinces and communities that had a strong native social structure, as any Christian community planted there would be marginalized by the larger community. They would be cut off from the resources needed to become places of influence. Instead, Paul focused on the Greek cities that separated resources from religion. These were places where new ideas were accepted and their melting pot of people provided unlimited potential for the spread of the Gospel.

The following key factors are common to nearly all of Paul's church plants. Whether he was actually looking for them or was drawn to the environment that resulted from them is a matter of conjecture, but it must be noted that there were many other cities displaying these characteristics in Asia Minor that Paul did *not* target. We conclude, then, that his goal was to establish key centers in an area and then release their members to accomplish the task of evangelizing from that location.

Paul Bypassed the Native Provinces

The native system could best be described as closed. The presiding priests exercised complete control over all resources and dictated what happened and what did not. The thinking of the people was strongly influenced by the few in leadership. Influencing this system would have been difficult compared to the opportunities afforded by the Greek city-state. Any converts in the native system would be considered a threat to the stability and life of the whole community and would have been dealt with. Since all resources were tied up with the temple, any churches established there would have had few resources to invest in evangelism. In fact, their focus would have been on survival!

This was a time of change in the land. New ideas and ways of doing things were happening in the Greek cities, and those who were interested in change were making their way to these centers of opportunity. Thus, those who remained in these native systems were more resistant to change. Paul considered these areas to be low priority when considering the establishment of key centers to propagate the Gospel.

Paul also did not speak the language of the people of Asia Minor. We see this in Acts 14 when the people were speaking the Lycaonian language.

> In Lystra there sat a man crippled in his feet, who was lame from birth and had never walked. He listened to Paul as he was speaking. Paul looked directly at him, saw that he had faith to be healed and called out, "Stand up on your feet!" At that, the man jumped up and began to walk.
>
> When the crowd saw what Paul had done, they shouted in the Lycaonian language, "The gods have come down to us in human form!" Barnabas they called Zeus, and Paul they called Hermes because he was the chief speaker. The priest of Zeus, whose temple was just outside the city, brought bulls and wreaths to the city gates because he and the crowd wanted to offer sacrifices to them.

But when the apostles Barnabas and Paul heard of this, they tore their clothes and rushed out into the crowd, shouting.

Acts 14:8–14

Paul and Barnabas were ignorant of what was going on until they were made aware of the fact that the people perceived them to be gods and were preparing to worship them. This language barrier, along with the cultural structure of the native system, confined Paul to focus on the Hellenistic cities. So his ministry was focused on his own community. He was not a missionary who left his own culture, learned a new language and sought to advance the Gospel within a new worldview.

Paul Focused on Greek Centers of Civilization

The places where Paul established churches were all centers of Greek civilization. Apart from the fact that Paul was comfortable in this situation because this was the world he had grown up in, these centers were ideal seedbeds for the Gospel. These cities encouraged creative thinking. In Athens we see Paul spending his time presenting his message of the Gospel, and the people, both Greeks and foreigners, were willing to listen (see Acts 17). Evidently the people did not see new ideas as a threat to their way of life, although those in authority would have viewed them with some concern. They would have seen Paul's teaching as undermining the god-status of the emperor.

While Paul was waiting for them in Athens, he was greatly distressed to see that the city was full of idols. So he reasoned in the synagogue with the Jews and the God-fearing Greeks, as well as in the marketplace day by day with those who happened to be there. A group of Epicurean and Stoic philosophers began to dispute with him. Some of them asked,

116

"What is this babbler trying to say?" Others remarked, "He seems to be advocating foreign gods." They said this because Paul was preaching the good news about Jesus and the resurrection. Then they took him and brought him to a meeting of the Areopagus, where they said to him, "May we know what this new teaching is that you are presenting? You are bringing some strange ideas to our ears, and we want to know what they mean." (All the Athenians and the foreigners who lived there spent their time doing nothing but talking about and listening to the latest ideas.)

Acts 17:16–21

In these cities the wealth of the community was not controlled by their religious system. Rather, it remained in the hands of the citizens. This fundamental difference from the native system meant that people were free to put resources into projects they valued. (This was the main way public amenities and educational facilities were financed.) Since the individual, rather than the temple community, controlled financial resources, the Church, as it grew, had access to money that could be released for Kingdom purposes.

The combined openness of the people in these places and their relative freedom from community pressure created an environment that supplied both people and resources for the growing churches. This made them centers of growth that, if the leadership were visionary, would have a major influence on the local province and beyond by identifying and developing bicultural people who could move in and influence Asiatic society.

Paul Focused on Centers of Jewish Influence

One of the characteristics of Paul's ministry was his focus on the Jewish communities that were found in the cities where he planted his churches. He seemed to target the

117

synagogue first and from there gather the core group for an infant church. Often a group would gather to listen to his teaching and, because of this, opposition would arise from the synagogue, often resulting in Paul's being forced to leave the city. One might wonder why he continued to use this method of planting the church when he knew by experience it would probably lead to his persecution. The fact is, Paul needed leaders for the new church that he was planting, and it was in and around the synagogue that he found them.

> As Paul and Barnabas were leaving the synagogue, the people invited them to speak further about these things on the next Sabbath. When the congregation was dismissed, many of the Jews and devout converts to Judaism followed Paul and Barnabas, who talked with them and urged them to continue in the grace of God.
>
> Acts 13:42–43

> When they had passed through Amphipolis and Apollonia, they came to Thessalonica, where there was a Jewish synagogue. As his custom was, Paul went into the synagogue, and on three Sabbath days he reasoned with them from the Scriptures, explaining and proving that the Christ had to suffer and rise from the dead. "This Jesus I am proclaiming to you is the Christ," he said. Some of the Jews were persuaded and joined Paul and Silas, as did a large number of God-fearing Greeks and not a few prominent women.
>
> Acts 17:1–4

> While Paul was waiting for them in Athens, he was greatly distressed to see that the city was full of idols. So he reasoned in the synagogue with the Jews and the God-fearing Greeks, as well as in the marketplace day by day with those who happened to be there.
>
> Acts 17:16–17

As God was preparing for the coming of Jesus and the birth of the Church, He laid the foundation in Jewish communities that spread throughout the Babylonian, Medo-Persian, Greek and Roman empires. Paul knew the history of his people and was well aware of how God had moved, both in the land of Israel and in the Diaspora. While the Jews were captive in Babylon the prophet Jeremiah had encouraged them to look forward, not backward, and become part of the life of the cities they were placed in. He said their future would be found in their involvement in these cities.

> This is what the LORD Almighty, the God of Israel, says to all those I carried into exile from Jerusalem to Babylon: "Build houses and settle down; plant gardens and eat what they produce. Marry and have sons and daughters; find wives for your sons and give your daughters in marriage, so that they too may have sons and daughters. Increase in number there; do not decrease. Also, seek the peace and prosperity of the city to which I have carried you into exile. Pray to the LORD for it, because if it prospers, you too will prosper."
>
> Jeremiah 29:4–7

Here we see a pattern that is well established in the Scriptures. God works through history, and what He plans to do today He has already prepared the way for. Understanding this principle, Paul was able to focus on the places God had prepared and thus was able to plant churches in a relatively short period of time.

The people involved in this previous move of God had created their communities around the synagogue where Scripture was taught. In contrast to the Temple at Jerusalem, these centers were open to Gentiles who came seeking the truth. A proselytizing program had led to a community with three distinct groups. First were the ethnic Jews who could trace their lineage to one of the twelve tribes of Israel. Second were the Gentiles who so believed in the message of

the Old Testament that they became proselytes, undergo-
ing the rituals required to fully embrace Judaism. The third
group were those people who found in the message much
that appealed to them but who were not fully prepared to
embrace the total system with all its rituals and traditions.
Scripture refers to these people as "God-fearing." This group
was the most open to Paul's message, which allowed them
to be fully accepted by God without giving up their own
ethnic identity. So, when the message of the Gospel came,
many found what they were looking for.

Paul recognized the need for developed leadership if he
was to quickly establish churches in the Greek cities he visited. His strategy was to target the synagogue, whose members had already attained an adequate level of knowledge
and understanding of God and His Word, so that he would
have a group of people who would quickly become leaders. Paul rarely focused first on people from a totally pagan
background as the length of time required to develop leaders
would slow down his church-planting efforts. He understood
that God's plan was progressive. God had already prepared
the right environment for the Gospel to take root and had
prepared the right people to become the foundation of the
Church. These Paul found in and around the synagogue.

Paul Focused on World Economic Centers

The cities in which Paul established churches were all
economic centers. This may not have been an intentional
focus on the part of Paul, but a by-product of his focus on
the Jewish communities. The Jews of the dispersion were
primarily involved in business, so the larger Jewish communities would be found in those cities that offered the
best business opportunities. The environment of these locations would have offered a great scope for the spread of the
Gospel. World-influencing cities were places where people

from many backgrounds congregated. These were forward-thinking places, and each became a launching pad for the Gospel to travel to far-reaching locations. Within the church of these cities, the Gospel could cross the cultural barriers from the Hellenistic world to the communities of the strangers who lived among them. Then it could effectively penetrate the homelands of these foreigners.

A good illustration of this process can be seen in the province of Galatia. If we look at the history of the Greek Empire after the death of Alexander the Great, we see the formation of several kingdoms of Greek origin in both Asia and Europe. Around 270 B.C. the Gauls (from what is present-day France) moved east into present-day Greece, where they fought several battles. Some of this army eventually moved into Asia, where they called the area they settled in *Galogracia*, which later became known as Galatia. Later, under Roman rule, Paul was responsible for planting churches in the southern region of the province of Galatia, and it was to the churches in this province that he wrote one of his letters. Even though Paul's focus was on the Greek cities in the south, it is likely that the Gospel flowed from these churches to the Gauls who lived in North Galatia and established itself among non-Greek communities, in this case the people of Gallic descent.

As a footnote, history tells us that when the first so-called missionaries from the church in Rome went into Gaul they found the church well established. This was because there were connected communities between the Gauls of France and the Gauls of Galatia. Because of this connection, the Gospel was able to travel naturally from one location to another.

The Success of Paul's Method

During the night Paul had a vision of a man of Macedonia standing and begging him, "Come over to Macedonia and help us." After Paul had seen the vision, we got ready at once to leave for Macedonia, concluding that God had called us to preach the gospel to them.

Acts 16:9–10

Paul's focus was on regions, not cities. So his call was to the *province* of Macedonia rather than to any particular Macedonian city. Paul's strategy was to target two or three key cities in a particular region and focus on building effective churches in them. It is important to note that just because Paul was in a key location, this did not necessarily mean the task would be accomplished. To be successful, the churches Paul planted needed to have the ethos of the Antioch church. They had to be passionate about the mandate of Jesus to reach all ethnic groups, to be inclusive of all peoples, to have a strong outward vision and to believe life and death were more important than being right or wrong.

Paul entered the synagogue and spoke boldly there for three months, arguing persuasively about the kingdom of God. But some of them became obstinate; they refused to believe and publicly maligned the Way. So Paul left them. He took the disciples with him and had discussions daily in the lecture hall of Tyrannus. This went on for two years, so that all the Jews and Greeks who lived in the province of Asia heard the word of the Lord.

Acts 19:8–10

From Jerusalem, and round about even unto Illyricum, I have fully preached the gospel of Christ.

Romans 15:19, ASV

When Paul evaluated his accomplishments, he looked at areas beyond the local city. In Acts 19 he stated that all the Greeks and Jews in the province of Asia had heard the Gospel. This was due to his settling in the city of Ephesus and staying there for two years to teach. He was not saying he had gone to every Greek city and town and preached to the Greeks and Jews in each one. But the church at Ephesus had raised up leaders who had traveled throughout the province of Asia and fully proclaimed the Gospel message. It is interesting that Paul identified the ethnic groups that had been penetrated. He stated clearly who had been evangelized and did not include the native people in his summation. This further reinforces the claim that Paul's primary focus was on the people of his own culture and that he was not involved in cross-cultural ministry. As early as A.D. 58, Paul could say he had fully preached the Gospel from Jerusalem to Illyricum. Thus, we know his methods were effective.

Paul's Method of Funding

In most modern mission work it is the responsibility of the prospective missionary to raise his or her funds from sending organizations, whether these are churches or friends. When the required amount of money has been committed, they can leave for the mission field. This is not how missions operated in Paul's day.

Today, missions is generally seen as the sending of a person, usually from a monocultural background, to a foreign country to take the Gospel and plant it in a new ethnic environment. We have located this cross-cultural activity outside the church. The New Testament Church, however, had its focus of cross-cultural activity *within* the church, and the people who went out to proclaim the Gospel were those who had already fully identified with their own people group. This may seem a small difference, but it does have implications for funding and maintaining the expansion of the Gospel.

When people are going to their own communities they have far greater access to resources than a stranger does.

They can also live the incarnate lifestyle that makes them more effective and less expensive than is normally the case today. They can also access employment and business opportunities that are not ordinarily available to those who are not part of these communities.

When we look at the early Church and the financing of its activities, we see an interesting picture. The first release of money was from a "daughter church" sending money to the "mother church." In Acts 11 we see the church at Antioch sending money to Jerusalem to meet the needs resulting from a famine in the land. Later, other churches that Paul had planted raised money to send to the needy in Jerusalem, but this could hardly be called mission giving.

> During this time some prophets came down from Jerusalem to Antioch. One of them, named Agabus, stood up and through the Spirit predicted that a severe famine would spread over the entire Roman world. (This happened during the reign of Claudius.) The disciples, each according to his ability, decided to provide help for the brothers living in Judea. This they did, sending their gift to the elders by Barnabas and Saul.
>
> Acts 11:27–30

> Now, however, I am on my way to Jerusalem in the service of the saints there. For Macedonia and Achaia were pleased to make a contribution for the poor among the saints in Jerusalem. They were pleased to do it, and indeed they owe it to them. For if the Gentiles have shared in the Jews' spiritual blessings, they owe it to the Jews to share with them their material blessings. So after I have completed this task and have made sure that they have received this fruit, I will go to Spain and visit you on the way. I know that when I come to you, I will come in the full measure of the blessing of Christ.
>
> Romans 15:25–29

Now about the collection for God's people: Do what I told the Galatian churches to do. On the first day of every week, each one of you should set aside a sum of money in keeping with his income, saving it up, so that when I come no collections will have to be made. Then, when I arrive, I will give letters of introduction to the men you approve and send them with your gift to Jerusalem. If it seems advisable for me to go also, they will accompany me.

1 Corinthians 16:1–4

When Paul and Barnabas are sent out on the first ministry trip from Antioch, there is no evidence that the church contributed to their needs or sent them any financial resources to sustain them in their ministry. Nor is there any mention of money being released for this purpose on Paul's other missionary trips.

There is evidence, however, that the churches Paul had planted released money to assist him in his ministry. This was not the sending church fulfilling their responsibility, but churches planted by Paul contributing to his support. Not that Paul relied wholly on this, for we know he worked as a tentmaker to meet some of his expenses.

Yet it was good of you to share in my troubles. Moreover, as you Philippians know, in the early days of your acquaintance with the gospel, when I set out from Macedonia, not one church shared with me in the matter of giving and receiving, except you only; for even when I was in Thessalonica, you sent me aid again and again when I was in need.

Philippians 4:14–16

After this, Paul left Athens and went to Corinth. There he met a Jew named Aquila, a native of Pontus, who had recently come from Italy with his wife Priscilla, because Claudius had ordered all the Jews to leave Rome. Paul went to see them, and because he was a tentmaker as they were, he stayed

125

and worked with them. Every Sabbath he reasoned in the synagogue, trying to persuade Jews and Greeks.

Acts 18:1–4

According to the book of Acts, those first missionary efforts did not depend on monetary support from the sending church. Those going could draw most of their support from the communities they ministered to, and so were free to get the job done without the problem of financial dependency.

Such dependency would have allowed what was happening in the home church to control what happened in the church plant location. So the new church would be affected if, for example, the supporting church had problems or decided to change its direction.

Today, our mission structure means the home church can dictate what happens in the field, as those who control the finances determine how they are to be used. However, if the home church does not understand the situation in the remote culture, they may not be qualified to make informed decisions about it. The New Testament structure also freed up the home church to release more people, as they were not limited in whom they could send by the amount of money available.

It is clear that Paul's strategy as documented in the book of Acts is as relevant today as it was back then. Paul's strategy included the targeting of key economic and multicultural centers of his world. These conditions are found today with the global movement of people. So the Church faces the challenge of how it should respond to the stranger we find among us. What should be our biblical response to the immigrant, and what rights do they have in our land?[8]

eleven

The Stranger among Us

Today, with the movement of people around the world, we are faced with new challenges that produce a variety of reactions from people within both the church and the wider community. Immigration continues to be a contentious issue. People feel threatened by others moving into their neighborhoods who look and live differently. Multiculturalism is a rising phenomenon that is intellectually embraced by many, but it can provoke an entirely different reaction when it comes close to home. More and more the non-Christian world is realizing it does not have the answers for the hostilities that are being created between people of different ethnic backgrounds. The mixing of people groups in our cities is not creating greater understanding and harmony but ever-increasing ethnic tensions.

In the Church we also face many challenges as we come to grips with this changing world. We have to deal with our own biases. We must move our churches from an ethnocentric worldview to one that embraces both the stranger and the citizen. We are confronted with questions about our rights and privileges as citizens of this nation and what protection we should receive because of them. None of us would argue that those from less-developed nations do not deserve to have a better quality of life. We are quite prepared to help them, as long as they stay "over there." It is when they come here seeking a better lifestyle among *us* that we react. Is this because their pursuit of prosperity might threaten our own standard of living?

In the Western world, we have a moral dilemma. We are 20 percent of the world's population, but we consume 80 percent of its resources. We set in place laws to keep out the "underprivileged" as much as possible, unless we need them. We claim that overpopulation is depleting the world's resources, and we shift the blame from our extravagant lifestyles to the increasing numbers of people in the developing world. As people seek to better their situations, many move illegally across political borders. Then, as they come into our communities and lives, we as Christians face a dilemma. They may be breaking our laws by entering our countries, but do we have the right to protect our privileged lifestyle at the expense of other human beings? Does the fact that we happen to have been born in a privileged country give us the moral right to deprive other human beings from participating in the same advantages, either because they were not born on the same patch of soil or because we do not want them? Which concerns us more: the moral challenges or the legal ones?

When people come from other communities, they bring with them their beliefs in addition to all of these other issues. We are troubled because they build their temples, mosques and prayer rooms in our countries. We are concerned that these practices will bring a curse on our land, drawing people away from the truth and destroying the freedom we now enjoy. We feel our ideals of freedom are being turned against us, and the values that made our land great are being lost.

But there are always two sides to a coin. With the challenges come opportunities. Today, just as on the day of Pentecost, we have all the people groups of the known world in our cities, ready and waiting for a move of the Holy Spirit that will transform their lives and give them dreams and visions to take the revelation of God to their own people. The key to seeing this possibility becoming a reality lies in the Church's ability to embrace the "stranger in our midst."

With all these issues facing us we need to develop a biblical understanding and attitude to the "stranger" among us. Much is said in Scripture about the stranger. Israel was always told they were a special people, not special in the sense of superiority, but special in being on display to the rest of the world, so that people everywhere could see what it was like to be in a covenant relationship with God. God intended that, as other people groups saw what it meant to have Jehovah as God, they would be drawn into the same kind of relationship as the Israelites enjoyed. God chose Israel as the firstfruits of a great company of people from every tribe, kindred and nation who would gather to worship Him around the throne.

When Israel rejected this calling, God raised up the Church. These are the called-out ones, a community composed of all people who live in a covenant relationship with the living God.

It is out of this overall understanding of God's intention that we must look at what Scripture says about the stranger or alien.

On reaching Jerusalem, Jesus entered the temple area and began driving out those who were buying and selling there. He overturned the tables of the money changers and the benches of those selling doves, and would not allow anyone to carry merchandise through the temple courts. And as he taught them, he said, "Is it not written:

"'My house will be called
a house of prayer for all nations'?

But you have made it 'a den of robbers.'"

Mark 11:15–17

We read here how Jesus entered the Temple and proceeded to remove those who were exchanging money and selling animals used in sacrifice. In explaining His action, Jesus reproved them for activities that had resulted in foreigners being excluded from God's house. In this we see something of God's heart and commitment to the stranger among us. The question we must ask ourselves is: What is in our churches that makes it hard for the stranger to enter?

God placed in the Old Testament specific instructions on how aliens were to be treated, what rights they were entitled to receive and what access they had to the God of Israel.

God's Anger Is Directed toward Those Who Mistreat the Stranger

Nothing provokes God's anger as much as our callous treatment of the vulnerable. The only time in Scripture when Jesus became angry was when He saw foreigners being excluded from the Temple. The Bible says that if we mistreat the foreigner, the widow and the fatherless, then God will let us experience what it is like to be in their situation.

"Do not mistreat an alien or oppress him, for you were aliens in Egypt.

"Do not take advantage of a widow or an orphan. If you do and they cry out to me, I will certainly hear their cry. My anger will be aroused, and I will kill you with the sword; your wives will become widows and your children fatherless."

Exodus 22:21–24

This is the word that came to Jeremiah from the LORD: "Stand at the gate of the LORD's house and there proclaim this message:

"'Hear the word of the LORD, all you people of Judah who come through these gates to worship the LORD. This is what the LORD Almighty, the God of Israel, says: Reform

130

your ways and your actions, and I will let you live in this place. Do not trust in deceptive words and say, "This is the temple of the LORD, the temple of the LORD, the temple of the LORD!" If you really change your ways and your actions and deal with each other justly, if you do not oppress the alien, the fatherless or the widow and do not shed innocent blood in this place, and if you do not follow other gods to your own harm, then I will let you live in this place, in the land I gave your forefathers for ever and ever. But look, you are trusting in deceptive words that are worthless.'"

Jeremiah 7:1–8

"Cursed is the man who withholds justice from the alien, the fatherless or the widow."

Deuteronomy 27:19

Today, in many of our Western communities, we are also starting to feel what it is like to be a stranger. In some states in America, Spanish is fast becoming the dominant language. There are many areas in our cities where a white Anglo-Saxon is totally out of place. We complain that certain races are forming ghettos—seedbeds of violence and racial hatred.

"Let's get rid of the ghettos," we say, but we need to understand how these were formed in the first place. The fact is, people gather in situations where they feel welcomed. The degree of separation that is maintained between immigrants and their host community is a reflection of the level of acceptance the host community offers the immigrant. The issue lies primarily with the former. If we want to minimize the problems of the ghetto, then we need to genuinely seek the welfare of these people as the Scriptures teach.

In Australia, even in the churches, there is an attitude that all these foreigners are coming in and reaping the benefits that our fathers worked so hard to establish. I was once talking to a woman in ministry who was upset with the lack of appreciation the immigrants had for the Australians who had built the land. Although her feelings may be justified, I would have to say that I see little appreciation from the Anglo-Australians toward the keepers of the land who came before them. As the conversation continued, the issue of concentrations of ethnic people in certain suburbs became the topic of conversation. When it was expressed that something should be done about what was happening, I asked her if she was prepared to sell her home and relocate to one of these areas. The conversation stopped.

In the same way, within the church the level of acceptance and genuine care we have for the foreigner is measured by their desire to be part of us. We are taught that people like to be among their own kind, and so they will eventually form a Christian community of their own. While this is true, a higher principle will override this tendency. That is, the principle of family! If we build genuine family relationships with the foreigners in our midst, we will see them integrated into our churches. This is because family takes priority. We may not always agree with our family, or like what they do. But we *are* family, and because of this depth of relationship we will stay together.

When strangers come into our community they are lost and are usually facing many issues. They may not know how to deal with those in authority. They may come from countries where authorities are to be feared, which makes it hard for them to seek help from such people. They also have the challenge of understanding the information that they receive. This is because when information is given, it has "assumed knowledge" attached to it. The person communicating speaks out of his or her own knowledge and assumptions. When the speaker and the listener come from completely different cultural backgrounds that have different core values and different worldviews, miscommunication and misunderstanding is not only possible but highly probable. Immigrants have basic language skills to learn, with the associated idioms and slang, and they have a desperate need to find a friend who will guide them through the maze as they attempt to live in their new world.

One time I went to visit the Omari family, recent refugees from Burundi, so that I could talk to their father. When I arrived at their home, the eldest son came to the door, because the parents were not home. I asked him to have his father give me a ring (colloquially meaning phone call) so that we could talk. Later that night I received a call from Jean Omari, who was confused about why his son told him that I wanted him to buy me a ring. Even small incidents like this illustrate the challenges that face the stranger.

God's command in the Old Testament is that we are not to "mistreat an alien or oppress him." His command in the New Testament is that we are to make disciples from all "nations," which, as we have seen, are actually ethnic groups. So Jesus' last word to His disciples was to take these people, who were not from the same culture as them, and do exactly what He had done. Jesus had made the Twelve His constant companions and friends; He had taught them and laid down His life for them. He then equipped them to go and accomplish the task He had started.

One of the conditions of leadership in the early Church was a disposition toward *hospitality*. The literal translation of the original Greek word for the hospitable person is "one who loves strangers," so a heart for the stranger was a priority for the early Church.

The Stranger Has the Same Rights as the Native-Born

Those who are first to this land have no special rights. I hear complaints from both Christians and non-Christians about immigrants who come to Australia. A common assertion is that when these people arrive, they should learn our language and take on our values and customs—adopting "the

Aussie way of life," assimilating Australian cultural values at the expense of their own. They believe that "because we were here first we have a right to dictate how the immigrants should live. After all, we developed the land, and now the newcomers are reaping the benefits."

History shows, however, that kingdoms come and kingdoms go. The Bible tells us that God sets the boundaries and times for the nations. We have no God-given right to this land, and we were not its original people. When the first colonists arrived, the Aboriginal people were already well settled.

When the early settlers came, they did not adopt the languages spoken by the indigenous people or their lifestyle, faith or values. The colonists believed that their own culture was far superior to the one they discovered. Today, we would still argue that this is so, but if we do, it goes without saying that every other culture will think likewise. In every situation the same conclusion will be drawn: The culture of those making the assessment will be the best. So why would anyone want to change? The issue of change is not an issue of national ownership but of national openness. Where people are open to each other they will feel free to discuss ideas and consider different values. Because they feel accepted, change occurs both ways. Where the host community expects conformity and openness only on its own terms, the result is resistance, cultural isolation, racial tension and inevitable conflict.

Scripture teaches that the stranger should be treated like the native-born. The challenge is to work this into our church life. None of us would consider not treating others equally—provided they abide by our cultural values and standards. God wanted the stranger to be influenced by the values He placed in the Jewish nation. Through this contact they would see the enormous blessings and benefits these values offered and would embrace them by becoming part of the inheritance of God in Israel. Then they might return to their own land and influence the nations with these same values. This mandate to influence the nations, which was the foundation of the Abrahamic covenant, has been given to the Church. How effectively we fulfill it is shown not so much by the number of people we send overseas on long- or short-term trips but by how easily the stranger feels accepted in our home church.

> "The alien living with you must be treated as one of your native-born. Love him as yourself, for you were aliens in Egypt. I am the LORD your God."
>
> Leviticus 19:34

> "You are to have the same law for the alien and the native-born. I am the LORD your God."
>
> Leviticus 24:22

> And I charged your judges at that time: Hear the disputes between your brothers and judge fairly, whether the case is between brother Israelites or between one of them and an alien.
>
> Deuteronomy 1:16

The Stranger Has an Inheritance in the Land

Here is something interesting to consider: We often feel negatively about people from other countries coming to our cities and buying up our properties. The underlying thought is that they do not have a right to our land. This was seen in Fiji in recent years, where the government was overthrown by the army because the Indian people had gained political ascendancy. The underlying thought was that only the Fijians, who were the original landholders, had the rights of inheritance, whereas the people who came in as laborers had no real rights. It is also interesting to note that the native

Fijians were predominantly Christian, while only 6 percent of the Indians in Fiji at that time were Christians. We can only speculate about what influence the violation of this biblical principle of equal rights to inheritance has had on the resistance of the Fijian Indians to the Gospel.

When we see Israel as a picture of the Church, the concept of inheritance takes on a new dimension. Many Christian leaders believe God has brought immigrants to our shores so that we can reach them, disciple them and then send them back to their own country. The implication is that it is not God's will for them to stay here long term; that is, *our* country does not need them but *their* country does.

> "You are to distribute this land among yourselves according to the tribes of Israel. You are to allot it as an inheritance for yourselves and for the aliens who have settled among you and who have children. You are to consider them as native-born Israelites; along with you they are to be allotted an inheritance among the tribes of Israel. In whatever tribe the alien settles, there you are to give him his inheritance," declares the Sovereign LORD.
>
> Ezekiel 47:21–23

If we allow the stranger to have an inheritance in our land, however, we will build connections between our churches and the communities these people come from. These connected communities are far more effective in moving the Gospel from one geographical location to another than the sending of an individual who has no roots locally. By supporting this inheritance principle we lay the foundation for an effective, ongoing relationship that will release resources and people and ensure lasting connections. Mission done this way will be more effective than sending an isolated individual home to plant a church among his or her own people.

The Stranger Has the Same Access to God as the Native-Born

The purpose of God is expressed in the Abrahamic covenant: that through Abraham every ethnic group on the earth would be blessed. The Old Testament is clear: Foreigners had equal rights to participate in the religious life of Israel. They were given the right to participate in the feasts that Israel was commanded to observe. They were directed to observe the Sabbath and entitled to offer sacrifices to Jehovah. There were to be no special rules for the foreigner or for the native-born. To God they were equal in status and importance.

> "'An alien living among you who wants to celebrate the LORD's Passover must do so in accordance with its rules and regulations. You must have the same regulations for the alien and the native-born.'"
>
> Numbers 9:14

> Be joyful at your Feast—you, your sons and daughters, your menservants and maidservants, and the Levites, the aliens, the fatherless and the widows who live in your towns.
>
> Deuteronomy 16:14

> "But the seventh day is a Sabbath to the LORD your God. On it you shall not do any work, neither you, nor your son or daughter, nor your manservant or maidservant, nor your animals, nor the alien within your gates."
>
> Exodus 20:10

> "For the generations to come, whenever an alien or anyone else living among you presents an offering made by fire as an aroma pleasing to the LORD, he must do exactly as you do. The community is to have the same rules for you and for the alien living among you; this is a lasting ordinance for the generations to come. You and the alien shall be the same

before the LORD: The same laws and regulations will apply both to you and to the alien living among you."

Numbers 15:14–16

Few people today would voice the opinion that some people are superior to others. Apartheid has gone, slavery as we knew it has been abolished, and the notion that Australia's own indigenous people are subhuman is no longer promoted. Today there is a widespread acceptance of our equality, which includes coming to God on the same footing. But the perception of our differences remains, and we prefer to associate with those who are like us. This attitude encourages the belief that the best way to accommodate all the different ethnic groups among us is to encourage them to create their own services in their language and style, so all can live within their comfort zone and approach God in a way that best suits them. Having done this we can relax in the knowledge that we have ensured equal access to God for everyone.

In fact, Israel did develop a separate location for the foreigners to meet in the Temple during the time of Jesus, and it had the effect of making them feel like second-class citizens. The attitude of the Jews toward the foreigners was clearly on display when it became more important to have the money changers and merchants there than to make room for the strangers. This may have been an oversight rather than a deliberate rejection. Any time we place something outside of our area of responsibility, we cease to consider it when we are making decisions.

The problem is that even though we have fulfilled our responsibility of ensuring that everyone has equal access to God as is made clear in the Old Testament, we still tend to see people in terms of "we" and "them," categorizing "them" according to ethnicity. In Ephesians 2 Paul declared that God's redemptive work would remove the dividing walls between human beings. This is not just about unity within

138

a cultural group. Paul specifically talks about the Gentiles and the Jews. God wants to break down the barriers that divide us by uniting different peoples to build a temple in which He will dwell. Paul's writings give little place to a separatist approach to church development. In Colossians and Galatians he declares that race, gender and status make no difference. This is not to say we are all the same. Paul clearly teaches that people have different roles and functions. He also urges slaves to obey their masters and masters to treat their slaves well. He does not expect slaves and masters to no longer exist, but he does insist that they are equally important in God's eyes.

> For he himself is our peace, who has made the two one and has destroyed the barrier, the dividing wall of hostility, by abolishing in his flesh the law with its commandments and regulations. His purpose was to create in himself one new man out of the two, thus making peace, and in this one body to reconcile both of them to God through the cross, by which he put to death their hostility. He came and preached peace to you who were far away and peace to those who were near. For through him we both have access to the Father by one Spirit.
>
> Consequently, you are no longer foreigners and aliens, but fellow citizens with God's people and members of God's household, built on the foundation of the apostles and prophets, with Christ Jesus himself as the chief cornerstone. In him the whole building is joined together and rises to become a holy temple in the Lord. And in him you too are being built together to become a dwelling in which God lives by his Spirit.
>
> Ephesians 2:14–22

> Here there is no Greek or Jew, circumcised or uncircumcised, barbarian, Scythian, slave or free, but Christ is all, and is in all.
>
> Colossians 3:11

You are all sons of God through faith in Christ Jesus, for all of you who were baptized into Christ have clothed yourselves with Christ. There is neither Jew nor Greek, slave nor free, male nor female, for you are all one in Christ Jesus. If you belong to Christ, then you are Abraham's seed, and heirs according to the promise.

Galatians 3:26–29

The New Testament teaches that our ethnicity is not to be a reason for creating division. Rather, the gathering together of many races within the church is an incredible declaration of the redemptive plan of God and is the greatest visible expression of unity the world can see. Through this expression Jesus' prayer will be answered.

"My prayer is not for them alone. I pray also for those who will believe in me through their message, that all of them may be one, Father, just as you are in me and I am in you. May they also be in us so that the world may believe that you have sent me. I have given them the glory that you gave me, that they may be one as we are one: I in them and you in me. May they be brought to complete unity to let the world know that you sent me and have loved them even as you have loved me."

John 17:20–23

Please understand that I am not against developing different language services. The issue is not the outward expression, but the motivation behind what is being done. If we develop separate ethnic services in our church simply because it is too difficult to change our own service or to change people's attitudes to accommodate the new arrivals, then we are taking the easy option. The dividing walls will come down only as we face them and see the grace of God working to remove them. If the strangers decide to stay within their comfort zone rather than embrace the biblical teaching of demolishing the walls, then the Church is still

140

building on a wrong foundation and will never reach the potential God intended. It is true that *"the same laws and regulations will apply both to you and to the alien living among you."*

The Stranger Must Not Bring Forbidden Practices

In the last thirty years the spiritual landscape of Sydney has changed; instead of churches, temples and mosques are dotting the landscape. Within the suburb where the Jesus Family Centre is found there are five major Buddhist temples, two mosques and numerous houses that have been turned into places of Buddhist worship. This invasion of foreign religion has been heralded by those in power as cultural diversification. These homes that have been turned into places of prayer are welcomed, but those who attempt to hold a church service in their homes are closed down. There is an invasion occurring in our land, and the Church seems to be asleep.

For too long we have seen freedom as the right to do what we like. We have been taught that we all have rights and that we all need to claim them. Yet for every right there is a responsibility. If we insist on our rights and neglect our responsibilities, we will eventually forfeit the inheritance given to us in this land. This was seen in the life of Esau and Jacob. Esau, the eldest son, was given the birthright but did not value it. One day when he was hungry after a hunting trip he was ready to throw away his birthright for some food. This was not a life-or-death situation, and yet Esau did not value his God-given inheritance enough to protect it. The Church has followed a similar pattern. Once, education was the responsibility of the church, but bit by bit we handed it over to the state, and today our education system has all but excluded God. This has encouraged a secular worldview that has no place for God and is hostile toward any reality beyond the natural realm.

Fortunately the Church is starting to take up its responsibility for education, but can it reclaim it enough to turn our Western society toward a more biblical worldview?

Scripture tells us God has a high level of acceptance of cultural diversity, but a low level of tolerance toward those beliefs and practices that violate His Word and damage His people. The Old Testament clearly states that no special dispensation is given to the foreigner to take part in unbiblical practices. God's judgment is equally against the stranger and the native-born if they do these things.

> "Say to them: 'Any Israelite or any alien living among them who offers a burnt offering or sacrifice and does not bring it to the entrance to the Tent of Meeting to sacrifice it to the LORD—that man must be cut off from his people.'"
>
> Leviticus 17:8–9

> "But you must keep my decrees and my laws. The native-born and the aliens living among you must not do any of these detestable things, for all these things were done by the people who lived in the land before you, and the land became defiled. And if you defile the land, it will vomit you out as it vomited out the nations that were before you."
>
> Leviticus 18:26–28

> "Say to the Israelites: 'Any Israelite or any alien living in Israel who gives any of his children to Molech must be put to death. The people of the community are to stone him.'"
>
> Leviticus 20:2

> "Anyone who blasphemes the name of the LORD must be put to death. The entire assembly must stone him. Whether an alien or native-born, when he blasphemes the Name, he must be put to death."
>
> Leviticus 24:16

We have given away our right to influence what is allowed in this land as we have delegated lawmaking to secular politicians. Regardless of our theology of government, the truth is that the Church now has little influence in determining what happens in our nation. In Australia, only 6 percent of the population regularly attends Sunday services. We worry that foreigners are bringing in their gods and thus bringing a curse on this land. But what is our responsibility? In Australia, every twelve years we abort a million babies, but within the same period we bring in a million immigrants. If we are seeing a curse coming on this land because of foreign gods, why is this happening? We have insisted on our right to choose, but we have neglected our obligations. By doing so we have given this land over to another.

The failure of the church to impact its community and shape the nation cannot be attributed to the influence of foreigners and their gods. In fact, the secular worldview of our Western society has infiltrated the Church and rendered it ineffective. As we have sought to rationalize the divine, we have removed from the Church the dynamic power of God to change lives and situations. In 2 Timothy we are told that this will be the condition of the Church in the last days. Our real task is to stop blaming others for our ineffectiveness and return to a biblical lifestyle so that we have invested in us the power and authority to impact both the citizen and the foreigner. The vacuum we have created is being, and will continue to be, filled by foreign gods.

> But mark this: There will be terrible times in the last days. People will be lovers of themselves, lovers of money, boastful, proud, abusive, disobedient to their parents, ungrateful, unholy, without love, unforgiving, slanderous, without self-control, brutal, not lovers of the good, treacherous, rash, conceited, lovers of pleasure rather than lovers of God—having a form of godliness but denying its power. Have nothing to do with them.
>
> 2 Timothy 3:1–5

What is the real issue in this situation? Are we prepared to take the challenge of moving the hand of God so that He revives our churches and prepares them to take the gates of the enemy? Or do we prefer to build a wall that will protect us so that we can live our comfortable Western lifestyle, with all the protection and security we believe we deserve, while His world is being destroyed?

Today, the Church is growing fastest in Asia, Africa and South America—all places where foreign gods are entrenched—while in the Western world the Church grows weaker. Why is this? There may be several reasons, but two stand out. First, the people in these other continents have a sense of need, and second, they have a strong awareness of God. Under these conditions the Gospel thrives.

God Demands That the Stranger Be Provided For

Those who move from one location to another are both vulnerable and open to change. When they move both geographically and culturally this vulnerability and openness is heightened as they seek acceptance by the new host culture. This is the time when the most impact and the most damage are possible. The Old Testament teaches us to assist the strangers and create opportunities for them to meet their needs with dignity. The tithe was not only for the Levites but also to meet the needs of the foreigners, the widows and the fatherless. In God's community, assistance was given to those who came in from the outside so they could resettle.

> "When you reap the harvest of your land, do not reap to the very edges of your field or gather the gleanings of your harvest. Do not go over your vineyard a second time or pick up the grapes that have fallen. Leave them for the poor and the alien. I am the LORD your God."
>
> Leviticus 19:9–10

> At the end of every three years, bring all the tithes of that year's produce and store it in your towns, so that the Levites (who have no allotment or inheritance of their own) and the aliens, the fatherless and the widows who live in your towns may come and eat and be satisfied, and so that the LORD your God may bless you in all the work of your hands.
>
> Deuteronomy 14:28–29

This concept of the church allocating resources to help immigrants and refugees as they settle in a new land is a powerful tool for outreach. In New Zealand in the 1980s we saw a wave of refugees coming into the country from Cambodia and Vietnam, and the government recruited churches to assist in their resettlement. This built an attitude of appreciation toward the church on the part of the new immigrants, and it gave valuable opportunities to influence them with the Gospel. Those churches that did not respond missed out on God-given opportunities that might have had far-reaching consequences for the furtherance of the Gospel.

We Are to Remember Our Roots—Once We Were Strangers

It is easy to forget our past. Most of us can look back and recognize that our forefathers came as strangers to this land. We in turn were rejected or accepted by those who lived here. It surprises me how quickly we forget what it was like. When I hear first-generation immigrants voicing their desire to keep others out, I have to wonder whether our desire to protect ourselves has replaced our compassion for those who are looking for a future and a hope.

> "Do not oppress an alien; you yourselves know how it feels to be aliens, because you were aliens in Egypt."
>
> Exodus 23:9

145

In the church we must recognize that we received the truth because others from a different people group were prepared to invest in us. We must remember with indebtedness how we received that truth and be ever ready to embrace the stranger so that we can fulfill our responsibility of passing it on.

The mobility of the 21st century and the mixing of the peoples of the world give the church doorways into the nations of the world. If we embrace the stranger, as Scripture clearly teaches us to do, we have the opportunity to do cross-cultural missions differently. If we did this, what could missions in the 21st century look like?

twelve

A 21st-Century Model of Missions

Missions in the 21st century need to change if we are to accomplish the task. One of the catchphrases I have heard constantly from mission leaders and returning missionaries is that God is doing great things in the world but we are not keeping up with the population growth. This means that in real terms we are losing the battle. I am not sure whether or not this statement is simply intended to motivate us to do more and give more. The problem with figures is that we can use them to say what we like, but if the figures people present are the truth, then we would have to agree that we are slipping behind.

To win this battle there are two different strategies available. First, we can continue to do what we are presently doing, but on a larger scale. However, it would be good to remember this definition of insanity: "Insanity is doing the same thing we have always done and expecting different results." Second, we can look again at our methods, clean the slate as it were, and start afresh with no preconceived ideas. Perhaps then we can come up with a more effective strategy to suit the conditions of this century. It is this option I want to focus on.

Never before in the history of humankind have our populations been so mixed. All the major cities of the world are multicultural, and in this fact lies the potential to reach the whole world quickly and effectively. The most vital factor in fulfilling the Great Commission is not the mission machinery but the local church. Until the Church takes seriously Jesus' mandate to reach all ethnic groups, and sees this as its main task at home, we shall never get the job done.

I remember sitting in a Gurung village in the mountains of Nepal talking to a group of young men and answering their questions about the Christian faith. We were sitting in a smoke-filled room, the only light being the reflection from the fire in the center and a few candles that were scattered around. We all sat on the dirt floor, and as my friend Gam interpreted for me, I sat and answered their questions. I marveled at what was happening as I was experiencing what most Christians would never have the chance to see. This was the very first time that the Gospel had been shared in this village! I had the privilege of bringing the Gospel message for the first time to these people.

Every time someone had come to the village with a request to tell people about the "Jesus way," the elders of the village had refused them entry. Yet as I sat there, I not only was given freedom to talk, but I had the privilege of leading the headmaster of the village school to the Lord. How did this happen? How did I, a pastor from the suburbs of Sydney, find myself in this situation? I had never considered that I had a "call" to Nepal, yet here I was visiting a member of my church in his own home and seeing firsthand what God was doing.

Gam had come to faith in Sydney and for a short time had been part of the church family. Because we took Gam into our church family, made him part of our lives and did not forget him when he returned home, the door of opportunity was there for us to walk through. This door led us to an unreached people group in a closed village, and because we were connected to a young man of influence in the village, we were able to enter as insiders, not outsiders. Even while Nepalese evangelists were refused entry, we could walk in welcomed by all the villagers. This is the potential of missions from a multicultural church.

The Local Church and the Main Task

The local church must take ownership of the Great Commission, that is, to reach all ethnic groups within its sphere of influence. This will require a major shift in our thinking. The church will have to admit it is largely ethnocentric, focusing intentionally or unintentionally on a small range of related homogeneous communities. In general, we have little understanding of our responsibility to the stranger and have been content to remain in our comfort zones, building walls of security within which we can enjoy what we have and at the same time being content to send out and resource those who feel called to cross-cultural ministry. This mindset must change. All Christians—not just a select few—are called to work cross-culturally.

The trend in the Western church today is to build churches around specific focus groups. We now have youth churches, street kids churches, oldies churches, ethnic churches and regular churches, which in general are white, middle-class in makeup—actually ethnic in nature. We seem to forget the Church is a family and, as such, it requires a diversity of ages, occupations and status to truly express this reality. We have seen from Paul's teaching that God wants to break down the wall of division between the different ethnic communities and make a new humanity. For this to happen, the Church must effectively include people of diverse ethnic backgrounds. When the Church demonstrates this inclusiveness and effectively disciples all people groups in its cities, we will have made it easier for the Gospel to travel quickly and effectively to every corner of the globe. In fact, no political or cultural barrier can prevent its dissemination.

In such a church two important processes will occur. First, it will produce passionate Christians who are also bicultural. Urban people from different ethnic backgrounds who become part of this type of church will develop their ability to live effectively within at least two cultures—their own and the culture of the host city. Second, the Gospel will move across cultural barriers and take root within the immigrant cultures that have found a home among us.

As a result we will see a major shift in the way we do missions. First, the process of moving the Gospel cross-culturally will occur within the home church where it can be effectively nurtured and strengthened, rather than occurring in a remote location. Second, as in the days of the early Church, we will have bicultural people who are prepared and available to take the Gospel back to their own people group instead of sending out people who may have little cultural understanding. These well-equipped bicultural people will need minimal support to get the job done.

Touching the Nations and Establishing New Churches

As the local church takes seriously its mandate to the nations, the Gospel will spread naturally down kinship lines. In the West we place a lower value on family than do those who come from the non-Western world. Because of this, people who come to our shores, whether they are refugees or immigrants looking for better opportunities, have a strong link to their families in their communities of origin. The needs of their relatives at home become their needs, and they give sacrificially to help them. They do this not under pressure or coercion, but because they operate out of a family mindset rather than an individualistic one.

150

When touched by the Gospel, these people have a great desire to see their relatives experiencing the same reality. This usually results in their communicating the Gospel through letter writing, talking on the phone and sending Christian materials for the family to read and watch. Through this action the first stage of preparation occurs and Christian awareness is developed. Also, the new settlers regularly travel home to their families, where they share their faith, and their family members likewise come to visit them.

These relationships, if developed properly, will allow the home church to have a far greater impact on the nations than is currently seen, especially in terms of the distance of outreach and the number of churches planted. Most of these cross-cultural church plants will flow not so much from the initiative of the senior pastor or the mission director at the home church, but from the people themselves. The church plants will be less structured and less hampered by budget restrictions and will bloom from relationships.

As the local church effectively reaches its ethnic communities, it has both the challenge and the opportunity to invest in potential leaders among the immigrant peoples within its fellowship. How well the church develops this leadership will determine its effectiveness in establishing churches overseas. In the New Testament model, Paul established churches and raised up local leadership. The principle is not just to send people out to pastor, but to send out bicultural people who have cultural awareness as well as the leadership skills and biblical knowledge to facilitate the training of local church leaders and to equip their congregation. Churches abroad can then be raised up, encouraged and assisted by the home church through its multicultural leadership team.

Working as Insiders, Not Outsiders

When Jesus sent out the 72 disciples, He gave them specific instructions. As we look at these instructions, we begin to see some keys for effective missions.

> After this the Lord appointed seventy-two others and sent them two by two ahead of him to every town and place where he was about to go. He told them, "The harvest is plentiful, but the workers are few. Ask the Lord of the harvest, therefore, to send out workers into his harvest field. Go! I am sending you out like lambs among wolves. Do not take a purse or bag or sandals; and do not greet anyone on the road.
>
> "When you enter a house, first say, 'Peace to this house.' If a man of peace is there, your peace will rest on him; if not, it will return to you. Stay in that house, eating and drinking whatever they give you, for the worker deserves his wages. Do not move around from house to house.
>
> "When you enter a town and are welcomed, eat what is set before you. Heal the sick who are there and tell them, 'The kingdom of God is near you.' But when you enter a town and are not welcomed, go into its streets and say, 'Even the dust of your town that sticks to our feet we wipe off against you. Yet be sure of this: The kingdom of God is near.' I tell you, it will be more bearable on that day for Sodom than for that town."
>
> Luke 10:1–12

In these verses Jesus says to look for "a man of peace"; when you find such a person, stay with him, as this will be the door opener. The principle here is that to be an insider will make you far more effective than if you are an outsider. An insider is a person who is connected by relationship, not necessarily as a blood member of the extended family but one who has been accepted by the extended family as one of their own. An outsider is a person who has no relationship connections with the extended family.

This concept is best illustrated by the Chinese. The Westerner's impression of the Chinese is either that they are very rude people or extremely generous people. Why the difference? It is simply this principle of being an insider or an outsider. If you are an outsider you will not be considered. In a bus line it is quite okay for someone to push in front of you, as you are an outsider; to the person pushing in, you do not really exist. You can be taken advantage of in a business deal because you are an outsider, hence the impression Westerners have of the Chinese as being unscrupulous. Yet if you are an insider, you will be looked after, valued and cared for; those in the extended family would not dream of taking advantage of you. Thus you will find that they are extremely generous people. This principle found among the Chinese is, to some degree, found among all people: We all have our circles of influence and relationship. What Jesus was telling His disciples was to operate as an insider, not an outsider.

The immigrants coming to our cities are looking for those who will be "lovers of strangers." As we welcome and accept them, we open the door to being insiders in their world, and when we go into their world we can minister from a place of influence, not suspicion. This gives the local church the opportunity to build numerous insider connections that are portals to cross-cultural mission opportunities.

We have experienced this principle time and time again. When Uong Nguyen first came to the church, he was welcomed as part of the family. Then when I traveled to North Vietnam, I was welcomed as a family member receiving the privileges and respect of this very influential family. It was as if the village in which I stayed was my home. It is of interest to note that this family has become open to the Gospel as it has come from the insider, not the outsider.

Using Relationship Connections to Plant in New Locations

With the movement of people around the world due to people seeking economic opportunity or fleeing war or persecution, the way we look at ethnic groups needs to change. Currently, with our understanding of the 10/40 window, we have a concept of linking people groups to geographical locations. (The 10/40 window is the area of the world that contains the largest population of non-Christians. This area extends from 10 degrees north to 40 degrees north of the equator and stretches from North Africa to China.) This concept needs to be replaced with a more flexible one that I think can best be depicted by the picture of an ethnic wheel. A wheel consists of a hub and a rim that are held in relationship in the same way that spokes hold a wheel together. The hub of an ethnic wheel is the home location of an ethnic group. In the case of the Amharic people of Ethiopia this would be their tribal lands in the horn of Africa. Because of war and famine, many Amharic people have left these lands and relocated to the cities of Europe, America, Africa and Australia. This has created Amharic communities far away from their origin, yet these communities are linked through relationship both to their homeland and to each other on the rim of the wheel. This means that in the cities of the world, especially those in the developed world, we have a multitude of these ethnic wheels that create a mosaic of connections between cities, the rim, and the homelands, the hub.

This concept displays the real picture of communities and identifies two important facts. First, there is no ethnic group that cannot be reached due to political isolation. Even if the hub of an ethnic group is located in a restricted-access country, there will be a rim community available somewhere in the world. It is these rim communities that have the relationship connections with the hub through which the Gospel can flow back into the restricted access country and start to birth an indigenous church movement.

Second, because the communities on the rim are connected, it is possible to use these connections to move from one city to another and gather open people to plant churches on the rim of an ethnic wheel. In 2006 Lokman Limbu, a Christian Nepalese in Sydney and one of the leaders of Jesus Family Centre Australia, traveled to London and connected with the Nepalese community there. He discovered that many Nepalese were open to the Christian message, and while there he was able to establish three small fellowships that have started to grow. This now opens the door to building churches from the city of Sydney in the city of London. These simple community connections by insiders illustrate how effective we can be in planting churches all over the world.

People with whom I have discussed this approach tend to raise two issues. The first is the "settling mentality" that churches experience when immigrants join them. The second is how we are to reach those people groups that are not found in our cities.

What about the "Settling Mentality"?

Many church leaders have observed that immigrants are not interested in giving up the good life they have found to return to their own countries to promote the Gospel. This has been termed the *settling mentality*. But the trouble with labeling the phenomenon this way is that we begin to think the problem lies entirely with the immigrants. In fact, the issue is more complex.

When we first came to Australia I had the privilege of meeting a distinguished leader of a movement of churches with whom I shared my vision of reaching immigrants with the Gospel and seeing them take the Gospel back to their own people. This would not work, he argued, because when immigrants came here they were more interested in enjoying what Australia had to offer.

We must ask ourselves, however, whether the problem lies with the immigrants or with the church. If it is primarily an immigrant problem, then the ethos and vision of the church would have little effect on their response. But if the issue is really rooted in the ethos and vision of the church, then we can expect to find different responses from immigrants in churches that have a different ethos.

As we have built the church in Cabramatta, we have seen a contrast to what is generally experienced in churches with regard to the immigrants' interest and passion for missions. We have found that immigrants have a passion for their people and are prepared to take the Gospel back to their countries. Some go permanently, while others travel home to build up the church by means of ministers' conferences, crusades and other targeted gatherings. Because we have experienced this within the relatively short life span of the Cabramatta church, I have to draw the conclusion that the issue of a settling mentality lies primarily with the church and not the immigrant.

I have also noticed that churches that have a prosperity ethos tend to create immigrants with a strong settling mentality. There may be two reasons for this. First, when this prosperity ethos is the primary value of the church, the immigrants, who are often concrete thinkers, tend to translate this as meaning wealth and possessions. So they will naturally focus on pursuing wealth. Second, Western churches are more conceptual in their mode of communication, which makes it hard for concrete thinkers to become part of us. So the immigrants we see most often in our churches have likely been educated in English-medium schools and in Western styles of thinking. These people often have a Christian heritage going back several generations, and because of this, they don't have the same evangelistic passion for their extended family back home, as many of their relatives have already become Christians, and there are active Christian communities they can direct their relatives to if they show interest in the Gospel message.

If our churches adjust in a way that enables concrete thinkers to belong, we will be able to reach a wider range of immigrants here in Australia. In our first-generation immigrants who come to this land from non-Western backgrounds, we see the greatest potential for mission; they are the ones who are closely linked to their families back home and have a passion to reach them.

What about Those Not Found in Our Cities?

This question implies that there are some people groups that never move away from home and are therefore completely isolated. But in my observation, it is in the nature of people to explore and travel. As I look at the city I have become a part of, and discover all the peoples that are found here, I find it hard to believe that we could not forge links from the cities of the world, either through direct connections or near-neighbor connections, with every ethnic group. It is interesting to note that there were Aboriginals from the north of Australia learning the craft of boat building in Singapore before the Europeans landed on this continent. Those who move are open to change and usually have strong leadership ability. They are the ones to target first. So my response to this question is, Could someone provide evidence of a people group that has no connection to a city?

The Role of the Mission Organization

What is the role of the mission organization in all of this? The approach I have suggested for getting the main task done relies on the church rising to its responsibility and seeing multiple connections developing between the church and the nations. We do this by using the existing relationships found among our recent immigrants. This approach would greatly change the role of missionary organizations and might cause some to feel threatened.

Because our current concept of mission sees "mission" occurring overseas and outside the local church, we have removed this function from our church arena. We have transferred it to the mission organization so the church can focus on reaching its local community. This has had the effect of removing from the church those people who have a passion for people of different ethnic backgrounds—the very people who are needed to build an effective, church-based multicultural community!

Many missionaries have become disenchanted with the church because they feel there is no vision for the Great Commission. They emphasize this by quoting the minimal amount of money that the church budgets for missions compared with that invested in the local situation. The reality is that the structure we have developed determines the outcome. The mission movement attracts mission-minded people and draws their focus from the local church. Even pastors who have a passion for mission may end up resigning and engaging in mission full time. So the people who are left to run things in the local church are those whose focus is on the local community, which usually means those of the same ethnic background.

How can we accuse the local church of having a limited desire for the mandate of Jesus when the answer lies primarily with the mission movement? Instead of removing the cross-cultural mission function from the life and leadership of the church, the leaders and senior missionaries of the mission organizations need to be taking up positions of influence in churches that have a passion for the nations. Mission needs to be brought back into the church. This will not be accomplished by itinerant missionaries coming to speak and to solicit support for their personal vision.

What the Church needs are mature, experienced and culturally sensitive people who will commit themselves to invest in a particular church to raise up a generation of people who have the ability to change the ethos of the church so that mission becomes the main task at home. These churches will not be raising money for outside mission. Instead, they will do mission at home, with the natural outcome of church planting in their connected communities.

Mission organizations have the skills and understanding that need to be invested in local churches that are serious about mission. There is a great need for input from these organizations, for they can build into churches an ethos that will nurture the immigrant and reach the stranger among us. Thus they will contribute to the base from which effective missions can develop. The mission organization must take up this challenge and return to the church what has been missing. Instead of pointing the finger at the church's lack, it needs to return to what it was called to do. Rather than being the instrument to fulfill the church's calling, it must help the church to fulfill its calling.

thirteen

Case Study One

City New Life, Christchurch

In the previous chapters I have presented a biblical model for missions. You may well ask me to provide some examples of these principles functioning today. Without fully knowing or understanding these principles, City New Life in the early 1970s had a mission expression that was fruitful and illustrates some of these principles to some degree.

City New Life was born in the early 1960s and grew under the leadership of the late Peter Morrow. Christchurch New Life Centre, as it was called in those days, was a dynamic, Spirit-filled church that had a tremendous influence within the community. Besides being a key influence in the charismatic movement of the 1960s and 1970s, it had an international reputation as a worshiping church and was known as a teaching center. This church is part of an indigenous movement of churches called The New Life Churches of New Zealand. It was a church that had a passion for missions and was involved in supporting many mission activities.

These included investing in the initial purchase of a property for the New Life Church in Poona, India, Bible school training and church planting in Indonesia and children's ministry in Thailand. Over the years there have been many ventures into the arena of missions, but the initiative that has produced the longest-lasting, least expensive and most significant returns in terms of connectedness came from the Asian Group.

The Birth of the Asian Group

The Asian Group began in the early 1970s through university students who were part of the Christchurch New Life Centre. At this time the primary organization supporting overseas Christians was the Overseas Christian Fellowship. The failure rate for Christian students returning to their homeland was 85 percent. That is, only 15 percent of graduates held on to their Christian faith after returning home. This prompted two young students to commit themselves to pray for God to change what was happening to the overseas Christian students.

As they prayed God showed them two reasons for the situation. The first was that the overseas students were not involved in, or committed to, a local church. This meant that they did not understand church life and had no sense of Christian community. When they returned home the pressures of living in non-Christian families were too much for most of the ones who had no church roots. Second, many of these young people had been dedicated in temples and given charms to wear before they left home. These were not dealt with, and so they lived under a spiritual cloud, not knowing how to get free.

Within the hearts of these two praying students a vision was birthed to see the formation of an overseas student group that was linked into the life of the local church, one that would see many overseas students come to a knowledge of God, be discipled and return to their nations as fruitful men and women involved in building the Kingdom of God. After two years of prayer, the breakthrough came. In December 1973 Pastor Peter Morrow preached a Gospel message at a Sunday night service. As was his custom, he gave people an opportunity to respond to the Lord. On this particular night he felt a need to extend the altar call. Time went by, and eventually, after half an hour, a young Malaysian man named Eric Ho responded by giving his life to the Lord.

Six days later, as Eric was jogging in Hagley Park, he collapsed and died! This was a great shock to us, and yet God placed a Scripture in my heart at that time:

> Samson said, "Let me die with the Philistines!" Then he pushed with all his might, and down came the temple on the rulers and all the people in it. Thus he killed many more when he died than while he lived.
>
> Judges 16:30

Just as more happened through the death of Samson than through his life, so more would happen through this young man's death than had ever happened through his life. A seed was planted for a future harvest of generations of foreign students, now spanning many nationalities. It was through Eric's funeral that a backslidden Malaysian rededicated her life to the Lord. Over the following weeks and months many more Malaysians gave their hearts to the Lord.

These students started meeting regularly for Bible study, prayer and fellowship. The Asian Group consolidated and came to birth in 1974, and students have been meeting together ever since. This group has never lost its focus and has seen many young men and women return home and become involved in effective missions.

The Sending of the First Team

In 1976 a vision arose in the hearts of the Asian Group leaders to send a team to Malaysia to be involved in church planting. A group of six young people rose to the challenge. In 1977 they resigned their jobs and spent a year in preparation, attending a full-time Bible school program run by the Christchurch New Life Centre. In 1978 this team relocated to Malaysia to focus on building the church there. The team consisted of Graeme and Lucy Fawcett, Chih Yunn and me, John Yao and Vincent Kong. Today, thirty years later, five of these six people are still involved in full-time Christian ministry.

This team first went to Malacca, where it linked up with a small but fervent movement of churches called "Latter Rain." For a short period of time they assisted in building these churches, but more and more they were drawn to the island of Borneo, the state of Sarawak and the city of Kuching, in Malaysia, which was the hometown of three of the team members. At that time there was no Spirit-filled church in Sarawak, and it was considered unreached territory. At the end of 1978 three of the team relocated to Kuching, and Chih Yunn and I returned to Christchurch. John Yao remained in Kuala Lumpur but eventually relocated to Kuching, where he later became the senior pastor of the church there.

The Birth of the Chinese Church

In the seventies, following the unification of Vietnam under communist control and the successful campaign of Pol Pot in Cambodia, there was a decimation of Cambodia's population. There followed a movement of displaced Indo-Chinese people out of Southeast Asia, to be resettled in Western nations. Christchurch was a recipient of some of these people. With this flow of Asians into Christchurch, and the fact that a number of the Asian students had chosen to make Christchurch their home, some of the leaders of the Asian Group stepped out to establish a Chinese congregation as part of the ministry of Christchurch New Life Centre. This was to be the first Chinese church in Christchurch. From a small beginning this fellowship grew, and it became the training ground for several young students who were later to go overseas and serve in the church.

One in particular who was influenced by this fellowship was Lim Gee Tiong, who today is the pastor of a success-ful Chinese church in Kuching, Malaysia. Also out of this fellowship a vision was birthed that sent a team from the Chinese Fellowship in Christchurch to plant a multicultural church in Sydney, Australia.

The Impact in the Nations

The impact this student movement had on missions from the church is interesting to follow. Because most of those involved were overseas students, there was an obvious move-ment of people from the church to locations outside of New Zealand. Some of the processes outlined in this book are clearly seen.

+ The development of church planting and the raising up of leadership from the Asian ministry in the church was not initiated from the church's senior leadership but from the Asians themselves and others involved in the Asian ministry.
+ The Asian students studying in Christchurch provided a source of bicultural people through whom the Gos-pel could travel into the communities of Asia and in particular Malaysia, from which most of the students had come.

- The Asian students were people with initiative, having a high level of leadership potential.

- The Gospel crossed the cultural barrier from the white New Zealand middle-class community to the Asian community via the Asian students who were studying at Canterbury University.

- The students then took this Gospel in a more Asian expression to their own country and established churches, took on leadership in churches and brought with them the Gospel values that, even before they left New Zealand, were already having a degree of expression in their own culture.

Many students have left Christchurch and returned to their own nations and beyond. To trace the movements and involvements of all these students would be impossible, but I shall mention the accomplishments of some whom I know about.

The first student who went into ministry upon leaving New Zealand and returning home was Roger Lo. Roger returned to Malaysia and now pastors an inner-city church in the capital, Kuala Lumpur.

In 1978 a team went to Malaysia and eventually to the city of Kuching, where they planted a church called Good News Fellowship. Graeme and Lucy Fawcett spearheaded this church plant and then handed it over to John and Joanne Yao. The church then developed a church-planting movement that radiated out into the longhouses and small townships in the countryside surrounding Kuching. Many churches have been planted from this mother church.

Graeme and Lucy Fawcett then relocated to Osaka, Japan, where they planted the Osaka Jesus Family Church. After handing it over to Japanese leadership they moved to Mozambique, where they were instrumental, under the initiative of the Osaka Jesus Family, in seeing a people movement develop among the Koti people in Angoche.

John and Joanne Yao, after serving as senior pastors of the Good News Fellowship church in Kuching, moved to Sydney, Australia, where John completed a master's degree in ministry. They relocated to Melbourne, where they are now planting a multicultural church in Dandenong, a diverse suburb of that city.

Jerry Dusing was the leader of the Asian Group in the late 1970s. After the completion of his course he married Lee Lee, a Chinese girl from Sarawak, and they returned home to Sabah, where they became involved in planting the English-speaking congregation of a native-speaking church in Kota Kinabalu. They quickly came into leadership in this church, and today Jerry is its senior pastor and the state leader of a movement of churches called SIB.

With the departure of Jerry Dusing and his wife Lee Lee, there was a change in both the leadership and the ministry ethos of the Asian Group. This new leadership had a high emphasis on training people so that they would be prepared to be involved in churches when they returned home. This training was in the form of Bible studies through regular gatherings and the use of camps during the student holidays, but there was little practical, hands-on training. I think the limiting factor of this period was that the leadership did not see itself as being called to full-time ministry or church planting, and, because of that, the people under them rose only to the level of vision they were exposed to.

It was during this time that some in the Asian Group had the vision to plant a Chinese church. Because these two initiatives were operating at the same time, some tension developed between them. The Asian Group focused only on students, while the Chinese church focused on the Chinese community, both local and overseas, student and non-student. The two leadership groups had different philosophies, and the Chinese church activities attracted more and more of the students who wanted hands-on experience in church planting and various other aspects of ministry.

The problem was solved by the wise decision of the leaders of the Asian Group to flow in with the Chinese church, and the two operated as one unit with the Asian Group becoming the student ministry of the Chinese church.

Under this new initiative of the Chinese church more people began to rise up for ministry. One such person was Gee Tiong, a student from Malaysia. He had been heavily involved in the Chinese church as a Mandarin translator, a worship leader and an excellent songwriter. After the collapse of the Chinese church in 1989, Gee Tiong became a key leader in the Asian Group and then returned to Malaysia, where he quickly came into leadership in a thriving Chinese-speaking church in Kuching. Gee Tiong is also a songwriter and has released a number of worship albums in the local Chinese dialect.

The Asian Group had started in the early 1970s with Roger Lo and myself praying and reaching out to Asian students. Then in the early 1980s my wife, Chih Yunn, and I established the first Chinese congregation in Christchurch, New Zealand. Two years earlier we had returned from Malaysia, where we had been involved in a church in Malacca. It was while pastoring this Chinese congregation in Christchurch that the vision was birthed in our hearts to come to Australia and plant a church in an Asian suburb of western Sydney called Cabramatta.

The Chinese church in Christchurch took up the challenge of this venture, and a team was sent in 1987 to spy out the land. In 1988 a small team of four adults and three children relocated from Christchurch to Cabramatta to plant the Jesus Family Centre.

It should be noted that these churches planted in an Asian context sprang out of a white New Zealand church. This church had a desire for missions but little understanding of how the Gospel effectively crossed cultural barriers or how to build connected communities for the advancement of the Kingdom. Yet, despite its lack of knowledge and its inability to produce connected communities, this church still had a measure of effectiveness in cross-cultural church planting. Its effectiveness was limited, however, because it had many features of the Jerusalem model.

fourteen

Case Study Two

Jesus Family Centre, Cabramatta

Jesus Family Centre is an example of a church that has functioned effectively in reaching, gathering and empowering the stranger in their midst. By making this their focus they have been able, without difficulty, to plant churches in many corners of the world.

Jesus Family Centre is a multicultural church located in the southwestern part of greater Sydney, in the city of Fairfield. Fairfield is an area that has seen a constant flow of immigrants over a long period. Since the First World War, Fairfield has been used as an entry point for immigrants since hostels were established here to give them temporary accommodation upon entering the country. The new immigrants would first come to the hostels for orientation, and after three months they were required to find their own accommodation. As those who lived in the hostels were familiar with the surrounding area, they tended to relocate close by. This meant that wave after wave of immigrants came into the area.

First, there were the East European immigrants and people from the Mediterranean who came after the Second World War. Later the South and Central Americans came because of conflicts in their own countries. Still later, after the wars in Indo-China, many thousands of Asians were relocated to Fairfield. The area has also seen a large influx of people from the Middle East, of both Muslim and Christian heritage. Today the hostels are closed, but the area is still used by the government to resettle new immigrants. Most of the new refugees arriving in Australia come from the refugee camps of Africa, bringing with them the color and culture of the African continent.

This part of the city of Sydney has an amazing cultural diversity, coupled with ethnic tensions and all the problems of people who are in transition from their own culture. Some want to stay in their familiar cultural environment while others want to throw away all evidence of their past in order to embrace their new country. The rest try to fit somewhere between these two positions. This creates problems of identity, producing deep-seated inferiority and role reversals where children can control their parents because they are the ones who can communicate. Inadequate language skills lead to failure and a loss of hope. When we add to this many different value systems, we have a breeding ground for gangs, violence, crime and a drug subculture. This is Fairfield, a city with great potential and great challenges.

It was to the suburb of Cabramatta, in the city of Fairfield, that we came to plant a church.

The Birth of Jesus Family Centre

Jesus Family Centre was born on Mother's Day in May 1989 as a church plant from the Chinese congregation of City New Life, Christchurch. The initial church plant consisted of a team from New Zealand—four adults and three children—along with a family who had recently migrated to Sydney from Malaysia. Eddie and Lee Peng Wong had been active members of the Asian Group in City New Life in Christchurch. They had met and married there, and it was through this connection that they joined with us to pioneer this church. Today six of the initial team who planted the church are still actively involved in its life.

From its beginning Jesus Family Centre grew slowly. This was due to the focus of the church on conversion growth rather than transfer growth. Growth was also hindered by Cabramatta's reputation, which meant that only those Christians with a sense of call would dare to come and visit. The suburb was notorious for violence, gangs, drugs and murder, and such a reputation tended to keep out all those who might have had only a casual interest in attending. Because of the slow growth we had the opportunity to build a strong community and firmly establish our ethos. As we grew we changed locations. From meeting in our own home we went to the local community hall and then to the local school. Later we leased premises in the heart of the shopping center, before moving to a large building that we subsequently purchased.

The Ethos of the Church

When we started the church we naturally assumed it would be Chinese, since we had come from a Chinese church in New Zealand. Moreover, at the time, Fairfield had 40 percent of the Chinese population of Sydney. But we discovered that God had other plans. We had intended to go to Hong Kong to learn Cantonese before coming to Sydney, but God said no—go straight to Sydney. Our first convert was a Vietnamese. God started to add people from different nationalities, and before we realized it, we had a church from many different nations. Out of this situation the ethos and values that undergirded the future development of this church were established.

Below are listed the values of this church, which have given it the ability to cross cultural barriers and gather people from many nations.

- We value Christian community. We believe the local church is an expression of the family of God. This is one of our most important values. The fact that we express ourselves as a family rather than an institution helps us to focus on relationships and community rather than programs and activities that people commit to.
- We value the mandate of Jesus to reach all people groups. We believe God has entrusted to the Church this mandate of reaching all nations. The Great Commission is central to the life of the church. It's not perceived as an activity that happens overseas but is part of our everyday activities to be embraced.
- We value the equality of all people. We believe that all people, regardless of race, color and language, are equally important to God and equally accepted in His family. God has no favorites. There is no class structure in the church, and no one is to be marginalized because of his or her background. All people, whether they bring much or nothing, are treated equally.
- We value the uniqueness of culture. We believe every ethnic group has within its culture a unique expression that adds value to the church, and together the combined expressions reflect the creativity of God in His people. No specific culture should have a monopoly within the church. The culture of the church should reflect the sum of the parts. As the ethnic mix of the church changes so must its cultural expression.
- We value the grace of God working in His church. We believe it is God's grace, working in the community of believers, that causes us to be transformed into the people God intends us to be. People change only

because of the power and presence of God moving in their lives. God's grace is vital for lives to be transformed. God's grace enables people to change into the people He wants them to be and not to be conformed to the cultural expectations of others.

- We value the Bible as the inspired Word of God. We believe the Bible is the revealed Word of God and that God never contradicts His Word. The final authority for everything we do is the Word of God. This is the foundation on which we build, and it is our standard for measuring ourselves. It is not a sword to attack others with.

- We value the ministry of all believers. We believe God has given all members of His family gifts, abilities and resources to build up the church and to advance His Kingdom. Everyone has a part to play in fulfilling the call of the church. Ministry does not happen only within the church. More importantly, it happens in the community. To accomplish the task of impacting the different communities with the grace of God requires everyone's total involvement.

- We value building for the next generation. We believe we hold in trust what we have for our children. The church needs to have a long-term focus and to lay a foundation for the next generation to inherit, so they can accomplish the task. Both giftings and resources are to be increased and passed on to the next generation, just as the blessing and promise to Abraham was passed from generation to generation.

Reaching the Nations at Home

Jesus Family Centre is situated in the most multinational municipality in the world, and it has been able to effectively touch the communities that live there. Today more than 40 nationalities made up of over 82 different ethnic groups are found within this church, and no one ethnic group dominates. The leadership is international, and the church operates as an extended family.

The Early Years

Jesus Family Centre was birthed in a cockroach-infested house that required waders to gain access after heavy rain. But the church took root. After seven years a prophetic word was given to the congregation that later summed up its journey. According to the prophecy we had gone through seven lean years and now God was about to give us seven plentiful ones. As I look back on those first seven challenging years, I realize it was during this time the foundations were laid both in the church and in my own life. Key people were cemented into the structure of the church, and those who were not to be part of the church moved on.

Like any new church starting up, we attracted some people who were frustrated—frustrated because they were not receiving the opportunities they believed they deserved in their current churches. Others came because they saw we needed help and they wanted to assist. The problem with these two groups of people was either that they had their own agenda or they did not buy fully into our vision. This meant they eventually departed to seek a place that would afford them the expression they desired.

In the early days the church gathered many Malaysians because of the strong links the leadership had with Malaysians from the Asian Group in Christchurch. Some of the Malaysians who had migrated to Sydney from that group came and joined us, and later, through their connections, other Malaysians came also. This meant that in the early days the Malaysians dominated.

In the seventh year of the church, dissension arose over the issue of leadership, with a group in the church aiming to have the pastor removed. As a result of a subsequent split the size of the congregation was reduced by half, with mostly Malaysians leaving. In hindsight, this was the best thing that could have happened to the church because the people had to decide either to stay or to go. Those who stayed did so because they knew this was where God wanted them to be and because they had bought into the vision. Out of this event a leadership team was forged that was committed to the vision and each other. The platform for growth was established. The church was ready to move forward!

It was during the first seven years that key people came into the church but, like seeds, they remained dormant until the change of season. Then a harvest was reaped. Our first convert was a Vietnamese from North Vietnam who had seen nothing short of divine intervention in his journey to Australia. This man came into the church and discovered a personal relationship with God. He then grew in his faith and has become a gifted bicultural leader. Uong Nguyen comes from a scholarly family; his father is one of the last Confucian scholars in Vietnam, and his family can trace their ancestry back to the Mandarins who served the old Vietnamese emperor. Two other key people were added to the church at this time, both of them having been contacted in prison. One was a young Cambodian man who was involved in the gangs of Cabramatta, while the other was a Nepalese. Both young men became committed Christians and later added significantly to the growth and direction of the church. From these original seeds, and others like them, the harvest of the nations eventually came.

The Opening of Communities

When Jesus talked to the disciples after He had spoken to the Samaritan woman at Jacob's well, He said, "Do you not say, 'Four months more and then the harvest'?" (John

4:35). This was said in the context of recognizing that different people groups have different times of harvest. When one group is open, another may be completely closed. Much good seed has been lost because we have chosen, like the disciples, not to be interested in a particular group of people, or have been unaware of the principle of different seasons for different people groups. By not identifying the area of receptivity we may have missed out on the full extent of the harvest. In our multicultural cities the Scripture that declares the sower and reaper will work at the same time is truly fulfilled, and we have seen this principle of different seasons for different people groups in action as our church has grown.

The first people movement within the church was among the Nepalese. This began with a Nepalese lady who had a dream about my wife, and so she and her family came to visit the church to see if all was well with us. Some eighteen months previously our first Nepalese convert had been deported from prison in Australia to Nepal, and I had promised him I would come to visit. The day I announced I was going on this trip, this family came to visit. They were excited to have finally found a church that had a vision for Nepal and so decided to stay. Just before I left on the trip several other Nepalese started to attend, and when I returned from Nepal this group had grown even bigger.

What had brought them in? First, they recognized this church had a heart for them and for their nation. Second, some outstanding miracles occurred that impacted the key influencers in this group and, as they found a place where they were accepted, they chose to stay and become part of the family. Now, some seven years later, this group has become one of the largest groups in the church. Within it are many different tribes, most of them being identified as unreached people groups. These include the Magars, Gurungs and Limbus people of Mongolian descent who have settled in the Nepalese mountains.

The door to the Cambodians did not open through our Cambodian prison convert, mainly because he was young and came from a gang background. (Generally the community rejects people from this kind of background.) The movement started with a cry for help from a Cambodian woman. We had just returned from a vacation and received a midnight call. This encounter brought into the church our first Cambodian family, and not long afterward others started to come in. The door was open and the momentum grew. Today there are many Cambodians in the church, with several of the first generation and immigrants developing a passion for their own people and other people groups.

What happened among the Vietnamese was different. After our first convert we saw little growth, for various reasons. First, our Vietnamese convert was from the communist north, whereas most of the Vietnamese in this country have come from the south and opposed the communists. In addition, most of the ethnic Vietnamese churches were conservative in nature, and thus they were wary of us, believing we were a cult. This was because of our more charismatic style of worship and our doctrinal stand on the Holy Spirit. Also, I believe it was in the plan of God. Vietnamese are by far the biggest community in the area and if, initially, large numbers of them had joined us we could easily have become just another Vietnamese church. So for some time God closed the door, and this allowed people from the smaller communities to come into the church. Later, when the door to the Vietnamese was opened, the other people groups were sufficiently established, so the church could move down the multicultural pathway and integration was made easier.

The Vietnamese have seen steady growth and, unlike the ethnic Vietnamese church, we are seeing young, Australianized Vietnamese join the church as well as recent immigrants.

The most recent newcomers to our area have been people from the refugee camps of East Africa. We have been blessed by having an open door to this community. Today we are focusing on gathering these new arrivals as they settle into our community. They have been through much hardship, and when they come here they are still subject to discrimination from their peers, especially in the schools and colleges. Yet they have much to offer the church and community.

With this influx of people, we now have in the congregation people from tribes that, back home, were at war with each other. Yet they stand as brothers and sisters in the church family, worshiping the living God together.

Along with the Africans, another group has opened to us, bringing exciting results. This group is not an ethnic group like those we have just described. Yet they have similar values and worldviews. This group is the youth who live between two worlds. They are not yet Australians, but they are no longer Asians. These are the people who make up the Asian gangs in the area, who are involved in the drug trade. They have identity problems because they don't know where they belong. These are the ones who are finding a reality in the church.

This movement started with a young Cambodian man who, after prison, lived with us in our home for around three years. Later he returned to live with his family. After some time he disappeared from church, and I thought we had lost him. One day, after several months, he reappeared, bringing with him four young men whom he asked me to disciple. This man had returned to the people on the streets and in the parties in the clubs had found four young men who were searching for something. One of these young men was a Cambodian whom God was working on, and he became established in the church. From this contact a network of people have been drawn into the church, and weekly we are seeing new, young Asian Australians coming into the fellowship and being impacted by the Gospel.

Divine Encounters

As well as seeing different communities experiencing a harvest time, we have had some amazing divine encounters. When God opens a door into an unreached community, it usually starts with one key person. This I call the "firstfruits." We have seen this principle with the Vietnamese, the Indonesians and those from Muslim communities who have come to faith in Jesus. Usually this key person will come into the church and over time will be discipled. The process can take several years, but eventually that person is grounded in his or her faith, the door is opened and the process of penetrating this new community begins. Below are the stories of two such people who have come into the church.

Doors Open to the Uighurs of West China

In 2003 the congregation had gathered for prayer as we had called everyone to forty days of prayer and fasting. As we were praying I looked toward the door and noticed an Asian man peering in. At first I thought he was Vietnamese, as Cabramatta has many people of this nationality. So I sent a Vietnamese leader to talk with him. The next thing I noticed was that this non-Christian bystander was being invited into the prayer meeting. Personally I thought this would be the quickest way to scare him off, but I also noticed the man was not Vietnamese after all, and I had the strange feeling he was from a people group for whom I had been praying for more than two years. After the prayer meeting I talked with him and, to my joy, I discovered he was! Later I heard his story.

This man came from the west of China and belonged to a people group called the Uighurs, of which there are more than 7.5 million. He had fled China because of persecution and was trying to bring his wife and family to join him. Although he was from a Muslim background, he was open, as he had recently dreamed that he had found himself in a church. Because of this he had gone to the church down the road, the local Macedonian Orthodox Church. Not being able to understand anything there, he kept looking, and that day, as he walked past our building, he saw a sign on the wall in Russian that said, "My house shall be a house of prayer for all nations." He could read Russian and became interested, wondering if this was a church. Because of this encounter the Uighur man started to attend the church regularly. His English continues to improve, his wife is now with us and they have both become Christians. They are regularly studying the Bible with key people in the church, and God is birthing a vision in their heart for their own people.

Doors Open into the Middle Eastern Communities

For many years we have been praying for God to open the door to those from the Middle East. Recently a Jordanian couple in our church asked me to come and visit as they had an Egyptian pastor staying with them. Through this visit I was able to meet this pastor, and even on the first meeting and with minimal English a genuine connection was forged. This relationship has grown, and due to circumstances beyond our control this pastor cannot return home. Today we have people from Egypt, Iraq, Iran, Syria and Jordan fellowshipping in the church.

These are just two of the many stories about the doorways God is opening into communities. Through them the Gospel can flow to the nations.

Going to the World

All these communities that have come into the church are connected to the nations and tribes from which these people come. The next step is occurring. The communities in our church family are linking to the communities in the countries from where they came. This enables the Gospel to travel between connected communities. We are starting to see this happen naturally in our Cabramatta church. Also the different communities here are at different stages of this process.

The mission focus of Jesus Family Centre is driven by its members. Mission flows out of the life of the church and is not the function of any of its departments. We take the simple view that when God sends to the church people from a particular nation or ethnic group, we have a responsibility toward that nation or ethnic group. The converse is also true. God has not given us the responsibility to reach the nations or ethnic groups He has not sent to us. This view allows mission and church planting to flow out of the connections of the church, rather than be just the vision and desire of the leader. Those who have the connections initiate much of what is happening in mission.

Inroads into Nepal

Nepal is a landlocked country situated between India and China. The 24 million people who call Nepal home are predominantly Hindu or Buddhist. Until recently the Church has been oppressed, and conversion is still punishable by imprisonment. It is from this closed country that God has brought people into our church. With the coming of the Nepalese the door has opened to Nepal.

Our first contact with the Nepalese began with a man from the hills of Lamjung. We met him at an Australian correctional facility. It was here that he gave his life to Jesus, and he started to attend church when given weekend release. He was such a model prisoner that during the week before he was deported back to Nepal he was given special permission to attend our church camp, where he was baptized.

When he left Australia I said I would come and visit him within a year. Gam went back to his village in the mountains of the Himalayas and was the first believer in the village. Eighteen months later I made it to his village in Lamjung, met his family and was able to see firsthand whether this young Christian was still following the Lord. I was much encouraged by his heart for the Lord and his passion for his own Gurung people.

Because of Gam's witness in the village, a church was planted in what had previously been a closed community—all because of one man who had found Jesus in a prison in Australia, who became part of the family and had remained connected with us upon returning home. Today Gam is pastoring a small church that meets regularly in his village.

In 2006 I went to Gam's village for the third time, where I was privileged to open their first church building. I was able to see the transformation in lives firsthand. As it was during harvest time, many were unable to attend the special meetings, but just to see the people of the village gathering to worship and looking at the quality of the young people who had given their lives to Jesus made me realize that the simple seed of the Gospel that we had sowed into Gam in Sydney, Australia, had taken firm root in Gurung soil.

Miracles in Dharan

Connections come in many ways. Dharan is a city in east Nepal, which is the homeland of the Limbus, a people of Mongolian heritage who have settled in the foothills. Limbus from Dharan have moved from their homeland of Nepal to the streets of Sydney and have come to faith in Christ. Today many are part of Jesus Family Centre. Because of this development, links have formed with the Limbus in Dharan. We have sent two teams to this city to invest in the church there. This has led to connections, especially with the relatives of those who have become Christians in Sydney. Several of these relatives have come on visits to Jesus Family Centre, and relationships have been strengthened.

While speaking at a conference in Dharan, I was introduced to a Limbu elder from a remote area of Nepal. He invited me to come and visit his church, but I had to decline because of time constraints. It wasn't until much later that I learned the story of the birth of his church and its connection to our church. Lokman Limbu, a Nepalese and a pastor in Jesus Family Centre Cabramatta, was the first Gurkha that we know of to become a Christian. Through his witness many other Gurkha soldiers came to faith, and this led to his having to leave the army. During his time in the army he would return home and share with his community. At first there was extreme resistance to the Gospel, but today there is a church in his village and others planted in surrounding villages. It was an elder from this church at Khamlalung who had invited me to come to his village, a two-day walk from the nearest road. Because these churches were started out of Lokman's ministry, they felt a connection to us here in Sydney. This has led to the church in Cabramatta sending a ministry team to Khamlalung, which resulted in the first evangelistic and healing crusade ever to be held in that district. Bridges have developed through relationships, which have made the mountains of Nepal next-door neighbors to the streets of Sydney.

Connected Communities in Kathmandu

Young people have come to Sydney from Nepal, seeking a future. The hopes and fears of their families rest on these people. They hope for a future that will bring much-needed finance to families who often live below the poverty line. But they fear their children are going to a country where they won't know how to live, among a people they have never seen. In their own culture only the family, and possibly the tribe, will offer any care or assistance, so the family has a great fear for their children's survival in a new land. This fear is well-founded as many young girls are lured under pretence of legitimate work into the sex industry of Thailand. Today it is said that one-third of all sex workers in Thailand come from Nepal. When these Nepalese who move to Australia come to faith and become part of the church family, those back home are amazed. They cannot understand why complete strangers would open their hearts and homes to them.

This simple action does more than any preaching could possibly do. On my third trip to Nepal I was able to meet many of the families of those who had become part of our church. The openness of these families amazed me. They, who had followed Buddhism and Hinduism for generations, were without exception open to the love of Christ, all because of the actions of a fellowship of people in a far country who reached across the cultural bridge, joined hands and welcomed the stranger into their family. The connections between the Nepalese in Jesus Family Centre and the families in Kathmandu have led to several families in the capital of Nepal becoming Christians.

In November 2007 Jesus Family Centre Kathmandu was established. Usually when a church is started in Nepal it begins with a few poor people or people from the lower castes. The first service of Jesus Family Centre Kathmandu gathered over one hundred people, the majority being contacts from the Nepalese in Jesus Family Centre Cabramatta. As well as the large number of people, I was amazed by the type of people who attended. Besides people from poor backgrounds, there were many people of influence. There were successful businesspeople from the Newari clan present. The Newari people are the businesspeople found in the Kathmandu valley and control most of the business activity of the region. There were many people who were from Gurkha families. Gurkhas are soldiers who are recruited from Nepal by the British Army and are reputed to be the best soldiers in the world. These Gurkha families are well-off and are people of influence in their community. When I looked around those both Christian and Hindu at this first service, I saw firsthand the effectiveness of church planting through connected communities. I don't know of any other church in Kathmandu that has started with such a large number of people from such a wide range of backgrounds.

Planting in Peru

In early 2004 a young couple from Peru who had been fellowshipping with us had to return home, although they intend to return here to work with us in the future. Having returned to Peru, they looked around and saw many opportunities. This prompted them to plant a church in the capital city of Lima. This church has flourished, and others have started from it. We have visited these churches twice and built connections; a team of young people from the church in Cabramatta has gone and ministered, building bridges for future generations to stay connected. It is early days and, as with anything that is just starting, there is the potential for great growth and blessing as well as for disappointment and failure. Whatever results from this venture, one thing is clear: The doors to church planting around the world are no longer removed from a small local church. It is no longer the denominational missions department that strategizes, or the parachurch mission organization that comes to offer their services. Church planting overseas, from a multicultural church, is as simple as having mature, gifted members returning home with a vision and a connection and allowing them to run with it. Today there are eleven churches planted in Peru and a new church in Equador with opportunities to church plant in Mexico and Spain.

Building in Ethiopia

Our involvement in Ethiopia started when an Ethiopian family joined the church. Mesfin Abebe met the Lord in the Sudan, where he was living as a refugee. He came from an Ethiopian Orthodox family, and he and his wife were eventually resettled in Australia as refugees. Here they became involved for several years in an Ethiopian ethnic church. As they grew they found this church was not meeting their needs, especially the needs of their children, who were by now very much Australians. Because of this, and other circumstances, they eventually found themselves fellowshipping in Jesus Family Centre and quickly became committed members.

A vision was born in the heart of Mesfin to reach his own nation. This vision has motivated him to develop an organization that has legal status in Ethiopia and can propagate the Gospel, plant churches, be involved in humanitarian assistance, buy property and carry out any activity for the advancement of the Kingdom of God in that country. This has opened the doors to Ethiopia, with churches being planted, evangelists supported to reach into the rural villages and projects developed to add value to the rural communities. A strong partnership is developing that is enabling Jesus Family Centre to invest in Ethiopia. It has been initiated by Ethiopians whom we know and trust and who are totally committed to the church here as well as the nation of Ethiopia.

Partnering in Myanmar

As Burmese people have made this church their home, connections have developed with Myanmar. Through those in the church we have linked with a small but sound group of churches, and over the years we have established a strong relationship. This has led to a partnership where resources and ministry can flow to enhance the work of God in that nation. The advantage of having Burmese here, who have made this church their home and are not marginalized or treated as window dressing, is that they will guard what belongs to them. If the church truly belongs to them, they will not allow anyone to take advantage of the church. They are also the people who can identify genuine needs and can advise on how we can best meet them. Many people from poorer nations have a perception that the West has an abundance of money, and that connection with a Western church is like striking oil. By using the mature Burmese Christians in the church as the connection points, we remove some of the potential misunderstandings, as these people understand the thinking of their own people as well as the realities of life in the West. I have found this combination produces the best results with the least friction.

Assisting in Vietnam

No nation is closed. From countries that are considered "restricted access nations," such as Vietnam, we have seen connections develop. Students are leaving these nations to study overseas. Refugees have fled and settled here among us, and they have connections with their extended families back home, which allow them to travel back and forth into nations that are closed to people who are not of the same ethnic background. In addition, diplomats from "restricted access nations" reside in our country. These situations have opened doors to Jesus Family Centre, and currently there are students and recent immigrants from Vietnam who have become part of the church here. This has given us connections with both families and the underground church in these nations. God has enabled us to link directly with the persecuted church, and we have been able to fund church-planting endeavors, educate pastors' children, see members from our church travel and minister to the Church in restricted nations and translate Christian materials for distribution within restricted access nations.

Summary

These are some of the mission activities that are occurring naturally from Jesus Family Centre, and it is only the beginning. There are more opportunities developing than we can cope with. It has also happened with no budget and no "planned" missions.

No door is closed. There is always a way the Gospel can enter into a community, and there are always key bicultural people prepared and placed by God in our cities who can open the door to the communities they are connected to. Our job is to connect with their communities in our own cities and build them into our church so that they become part of us. Then the Gospel travels naturally via this connection to their communities back home, allowing the Gospel to take root in fertile soil.

This is not some unique experience that is happening in one particular church, but it is a model of missions that is built on the biblical pattern found in the book of Acts. This model can be embraced by any church that sees mission not only as God's top priority but also the church's top priority. As more and more churches embrace this understanding of missions and embrace the strangers in their communities, they can start to build connected communities around the world. Through this the Gospel will be able to travel to every people group, and the Church will at last be effective in fulfilling the mandate of the Great Commission. I have written this in the hope that it will cause us to rethink what we are doing in the light of the scriptural record and hopefully help us build a more effective missions movement to take advantage of what is happening in our 21st-century world.

Notes

1. D. B. Barrett and T. M. Johnson, "Annual Statistical Table on Global Mission: 2004," *International Bulletin of Missionary Research* 28 (1) (January 2004), 25.

2. Consultants: Harm J de. Bly. Michigan State University, Carl Haub. "Reshaping a Continent," Population Reference Bureau. National Geographic Society, Washington, D.C., April 2005.

3. Kim Murphy, "Russians Realise They Must Populate or Perish," *The Sydney Morning Herald*, October 21–22, 2006.

4. Piers Akerman, "Japan Confronts Age of the Last Samurai," *The Sydney Daily Telegraph*, June 27, 2006.

5. Gerard Wright, "Land of the Free Fills Up," *The Sydney Morning Herald*, October 14–15, 2006.

6. Immigration statistics, OECD, http://www.nationmaster.com/graph/imm_for_pop-immigration-foreign-population.

7. Lausanne 1974, International Congress on World Evangelism, http://www.ichenetwork.org/P12_P13.pdf.

8. In this chapter, I have drawn material and developed some thoughts from Roland Allen's book *Missionary Methods: St. Paul's or Ours?* (Grand Rapids: Eerdmans, 1962). To this, I have added other thoughts and material, but I am indebted to the author for his teaching in this book.

Index

Abebe, Mesfin, 187–88
abortion, 17–18
Abrahamic covenant, 135, 137
Acts
  on biculturalism, 23
  and clash of cultures, 27–30
  missions mandate of, 42, 190
African Americans, 11
Africans, 180
Alexander the Great, 39, 74, 121
alien. *See* stranger
Allen, Roland, 191n8
Amharic communities, 154
Ananias, 55
Ananias and Sapphira, 66
Angoche, 166
Antioch church, 36, 48, 52–56, 71,
  74–83, 93–94, 111, 124
Antiochus Seleucus, 74
Apartheid, 138
Asia Minor, 111–12, 115
Asian Group, 162–68, 173, 176
Asian students, 165–66
Australia
  birth rate, 18
  on foreigners, 131–32, 133–34
  indigenous people, 138
  influence of church in, 143

Babylon, 39, 119
Balcombe, Dennis and Kathy, 98
Barnabas, 27, 36, 53–57, 69, 75, 76,
  78, 81
barriers. *See* cultural barriers
biases, 127
Bible
  authority of, 175
  on the stranger, 129
biblical worldview, 142
biculturalism, 40, 42, 57, 82, 85–94,
  150, 165
birth rates, 17–18
Boyd, Chih Yunn, 19, 72, 99, 164, 168
Boyd, David, 12
bridge building, 40–42
Buddhism, 141, 183, 186
Burmese, 188–89

Cabramatta, 41, 168, 172–73
calling, 96, 109
Cambodia, Cambodians, 164, 179, 180
Canaanite woman, 63
Canterbury University, 166
Carmichael, Amy, 108
cell groups, 21
centurion, 63–64
change, openness to, 144

children, 175
  learning values, 103
  of missionaries, 96
China, Chinese, 72–73, 153, 164–65, 167
Cho, Yonggi, 21
Christchurch, New Zealand, 19, 72, 98, 168
church, 129
  and education, 142
  as family, 104, 149, 174
  impacts community, 143–44
  as institution, 102–4
  mobilized for mission, 101
  in multicultural society, 11
  unity of, 140
cities
  becoming multiethnic, 18
  growth of, 112
  links through, 157
  Paul's focus on, 120–21
City New Life, Christchurch, 19, 109, 161, 164, 165, 172–73
civilization, centers of, 116–17
colonization, 134
comfort zones, 42, 52, 73, 82, 93–94, 102, 106, 140, 149
community, 65–66, 154, 174
conflict, of cultures, 27–30
core values, 22, 59, 90, 132
  of Antioch church, 75–81
  of Jerusalem church, 64–73
Cornelius, 32–33, 51, 54, 67, 69
cross-cultural conflict. *See* conflict, of cultures
cross-cultural ministry, 20, 40, 85, 86, 106, 149
cult mentality, 66
cultural awareness, 82
cultural barriers, 49, 56, 139
culture, uniqueness of, 174
customs, 81
cycles, in church planting, 21–22
Cyprus, 53
Cyrus, 39

Damascus, 48, 55
daughter church, 124

developed world, 17
Dharan, 184–85
Diaspora, 40, 119
disciples, 60–61
discipleship, 21, 26, 102–6
dispersion, 68, 120
divine encounters, 181–82
dress, 30
drug trade, 180
Dusing, Jerry, 167

East Africans, 30, 180
economic centers, 120–21
education, 141–42
Egypt, 182
Ephesus, 122–23
Equador, 187
equality, 138, 174
Esau and Jacob, 141
Ethiopia, Ethiopians, 35–36, 49, 50, 187–88
ethnic churches, 93, 106
ethnicity, 26, 49, 80, 138–40, 149, 154–55
ethnocentrism, 127, 138–40, 149
ethnos, 26
Europe, population decline, 17–18
evangelism, 31–33, 50
extended family, 153

Fairfield, 171–72, 173
family platform, in church, 105
family relationships, 150–51
  with stranger, 132
famine, in Jerusalem, 73–74, 124
fatherless, 144
Fawcett, Graeme and Lucy, 164, 166
Fiji, 135–36
financial dependency, 126
firstfruits, 181
foreign gods, 143–44
foreigner. *See* stranger
Fuller Theological Seminary, 12

G12, 21
Galatia, 121
Gamaliel, 88, 89

Gentiles, 29, 51–52, 60–70, 63
God, works through history, 119
God-fearing, 120
going, vs. moving, 102
gospel, 29
    and cultural barriers, 20–21, 150
    resistance to, 30
    spread of, 48–49
grace, 66, 70, 174–75
Great Commission, 12–13, 17, 18, 60,
    102, 105–6, 190
    central to life of church, 174
    and church at Antioch, 82
    and local church, 148, 149, 158–59
    vision for, 158
Greco-Roman culture, 40, 49, 51–57, 90
Greek city-state, 111–12, 115, 116
Greek Empire, 119
Gurkhas, 186
Gurungs, 178

harvest, 62–63, 77–78, 178
Harvest Rock Church (Los Angeles),
    12–13
Hebraic Jews, 43–48, 51, 64, 71–72, 108
Hellenistic Jews, 34–37, 39–40, 42,
    43–48, 50–51, 56–57
heresy, 79
Himalayan Mountains, 41
Hinduism, 183, 186
Ho, Eric, 163
Holy Spirit, 51
homogeneous churches, 12, 92, 149
hospitality, 133
host culture, 49

immigrants, 18, 93, 132, 145, 150,
    155–57, 158, 171–72
immortality, 79
incarnate principle, 96–99, 124
inclusiveness, in the church, 149
indigenous church movement, 155
individualism, 96–97, 109, 150
inflexibility, 69–71, 73
inheritance, 135–36
insiders and outsiders, 152–53

International Congress on World
    Evangelism (1974), 31
Iran, 182
Iraq, 182
Israel, 61

Japan, 18
Jerusalem church, 27–29, 43–48,
    53–54, 59–74, 82–83, 94
Jesus
    cleaning out of Temple, 61–62
    on discipleship, 104
    on marriage, 79
    as missionary, 95, 99
Jesus Family Centre, 141, 168, 171–90
Jewish communities, in Paul's mission-
    ary journeys, 117–20
John, 48
Jordan, 182
Judea, 33–34, 37

Kathmandu, 185–87
kingdom, establishment of, 60–61,
    77–78
King, Martin Luther, 11
Kong, Vincent, 164
Kota Kinabalu, 167
Koti people, 166
Kuala Lumpur, 164, 166
Kuching, Malaysia, 164, 165, 166, 167,
    168, 194

Lamjung, 183–84
language barrier, 116, 140
Latin community, 11
"Latter Rain", 164
law, 64, 66
leadership, 71–73, 176–77
    in Antioch, 76–78
    in Jerusalem, 53–54, 82–83, 94
life and death, 79
lifestyle, 70, 79, 108
Limbu, Lokman, 155, 185
Limbus, 178, 184
local church
    and Great Commission, 148, 149,
    158–59
    and missions, 107

Lo, Roger, 166, 168
London, 19, 155
Los Angeles, 11, 13
Lucius of Cyrene, 76
Luke, 49, 57, 111

Magars, 41, 178
Malaysia, Malaysians, 164, 166, 168, 176–77
Manaen, 76, 77
mandate, for missions, 42, 101–6
Mark, 57, 108
marriage, 79
Medo-Persian Empire, 39, 119
Mexico, 187
Middle East, 182
migration, 18
ministry, of all believers, 175
mission organizations, 157–59
missionaries, 20, 96
missions
   emotive response to, 107–10
   funding of, 123–26
   and local church, 107, 183
   mandate for, 42, 101–6
   shaped by Western world, 96
   in 21st century, 147, 190
   mobility, of 21st century, 144–46
Mongolian people, 41, 178, 184
monoculturalism, 28, 40, 42, 62, 63, 68, 86, 92, 108
   inflexibility of, 69–71
Morrow, Peter, 161, 163
mother church, 124
multicultural churches, 23, 78–79, 86, 94
multiculturalism, 11, 42, 127
Myanmar, 188–89

nations, 26
   in Abrahamic covenant, 135
   as ethnic groups, 101, 133
   reaching of, 23
native system, 115–16, 117
Nepal, Nepalese, 41, 148–49, 155, 178, 183–86

New Life Centre Christchurch. *See* City New Life, Christchurch
New Zealand, 18, 19–20
Newari, 186
Nguyen, Uong, 91–92, 153, 177

Osaka, Japan, 166
overpopulation, 128
Overseas Christian Fellowship, 162

paganism, 79
Paris, 19
Paul, 27
   as bicultural, 86–90, 94
   call to Gentiles, 56, 67, 89, 139
   confronts Peter, 80–81
   conversion of, 54
   influence in Antioch, 78
   on marriage, 79
   method of funding, 123–26
   as Pharisee, 46–47
   strategy for church expansion, 111–26
Pentecost, 43
perceived call, 109
persecution, 33, 46, 68
Peru, 187
Peter, 48–49
   focus on Jewish people, 67
   visit to Cornelius, 32–33, 51–52, 67, 69
Pharisees, 46–47, 64
Philip, 34, 35–36, 48, 51
polygamy, 79
population growth, 147
potted plants, vs. transplants, 97
proselytes, 120
prosperity, 156
purpose-driven churches, 21

racism, 12, 131
refugees, 145
relational lifestyle, 104–6
rights, of strangers, 133–34
rim communities, 154
Roman Empire, 39, 50, 74, 88, 119
ruling, 67–69
Russia, 17–18
"Ruth" principle, 98

196

Samaria, Samaritans, 34, 37, 48–49, 50
Samaritan woman, 62, 64, 177
Samson, 163
Saul, 54–57, 89. *See also* Paul
second-class citizens, 46, 138
secular worldview, 141–42
seeker-sensitive churches, 21
Seleucia, 74
settling mentality, 155–57
sex industry, 185–86
short-term mission mentality, 98–99
SIB, 167
signs and wonders, 65
Silas, 71
Simeon Niger, 76
slaves, slavery, 138, 139
Spain, 187
Spanish language, 131
Stephen, 44, 46–47, 48, 52
stranger, 127–46, 149, 153
Sydney, 19, 41, 155, 167, 171–72
synagogues, 39, 44, 118–20
Syria, 182

target culture, 49
Tarsus, 88–89
Taylor, Hudson, 108
Temple, 44, 61–62
10/40 window, 154
Thailand, 185–86
thistle, seed head of, 19
Timothy, 57

Tiong, Lim Gee, 165, 168
traditions, 29

Uighurs, 181–82
underdeveloped world, 17
urban poor, 17, 18
urbanization, 17

values, 103
Vietnam, Vietnamese, 32, 164, 177, 179, 181, 189
violence, 131
visionary churches, 77, 114
vulnerability, 144

wall of division, 149
wealth, 156
western culture
    consumption of, 128
    individualism of, 96–97, 109, 150
    racism in, 11–12
    shaped mission, 96
    style of dress, 30
    on success, 21
    worldview of, 102–3
widows, 144
Wong, Eddie and Lee Peng, 173
world vision, 13
worldview, 88–89, 93–94
worship, 44

Yao, John and Joanne, 164, 167–68

David Boyd was born in Lower Hutt, New Zealand, and then moved to Christchurch at the age of two, where he grew up. He was educated in a Christian school called Middleton Grange, where he overcame a reading disability called dyslexia, and in 1970 went on to study at Canterbury University. Here he completed a bachelor's degree in science, majoring in zoology. In 1973 he completed a postgraduate diploma in natural resources and then went on to work as a pedologist (soil scientist) for the Department of Scientific and Industrial Research (DSIR). In 1977 David resigned from his position with the DSIR to attend the Bible college associated with his local church, New Life Centre Christchurch, where he completed a diploma in pastoral ministry.

David was born into a churchgoing family and, at the age of twelve, came to faith in Jesus Christ. In 1968, at the height of the charismatic renewal, David was baptized in the Holy Spirit and became involved in the New Life Centre in Christchurch, New Zealand. In 1972 David was instrumental in establishing and leading, for many years, a church-based overseas student organization that had significant impact on the Malaysian and Singaporean students studying in Christchurch. This group has continued to this day as a strong influence among overseas students in Christchurch. It has been instrumental in raising up many leaders who have returned to their own countries as pastors and Christian leaders. Some today are leaders of denominations in their own countries, and these leaders are having significant impact in many countries of Asia.

In 1972 Wu Chih Yunn traveled from Kuching, Malaysia, to Christchurch, New Zealand, where she enrolled in Canterbury University for a bachelor's of commerce degree, which she completed in 1974. In 1974 Chih Yunn gave her life to Jesus and became a committed member of New Life Centre Christchurch. David and Chih Yunn met through their involvement in the Asian ministry in the local church, and in 1977 they were married and attended Bible school together.

In 1978 David and Chih Yunn traveled to Malaysia for a year with a team to be involved in church planting and ministry. Much of their time was spent in Malacca assisting a young pastor, as well as seeing the foundation laid for a church plant in Kuching, Sarawak, which has grown into a movement of churches in the state of Sarawak.

In 1979 David and Chih Yunn returned to Christchurch and became involved again in overseas student ministry. In 1984 they stepped out to establish the first Chinese church in Christchurch to gather the local Chinese and the recent immigrants from Vietnam and Cambodia who were settling in Christchurch. This church grew to around one hundred people, which was around 5 percent of the total Chinese population of the city. This church had people from many Asian nations attending.

In 1989 David and Chih Yunn handed the church over to a Singaporean couple and relocated to Sydney, Australia, with two other young ladies to pioneer a new church in Cabramatta. Cabramatta at that time was part of the most multicultural local government region in the world. This church has become a dynamic multicultural church, made up of over 82 different ethnic groups, and has an attendance of over 500 people. All continents are represented in this church, and the church operates as a family that crosses the cultural barriers, allowing people to develop genuine relationships.

David has ministered and traveled in many nations, including Peru, Argentina, Ethiopia, India, Nepal, Myanmar, Thailand, Vietnam, Cambodia, Laos, Malaysia, Singapore, Indonesia, Canada and the United States.

From many years of cross-cultural ministry, he presents in this book some challenging insights into the dynamics of mission and cross-cultural ministry from his own experience and the Word of God.

The Boyds have three children, Nathan, Peter and Amy, who are actively involved in the life and ministry of the church. Nathan and Peter (twins) have completed their accounting degrees and are working for accounting firms as well as taking leadership responsibilities in the church. Amy is at a university majoring in accounting. David is the senior pastor of the Jesus Family Centre, leading a multicultural pastoral team and staff who come from New Zealand, Vietnam, Myanmar, Brazil, Nepal, Indonesia and Peru. Chih Yunn is actively involved in the church as well as running her own accountancy.

David and the church are focused on church planting and are looking to plant churches in the communities that members of the church have come from. Also they seek to identify key cities such as Los Angeles, Paris and London where multicultural churches could be planted that would be able to make a significant contribution to missions. To this end, several senior members of the church are traveling to both America and Europe to develop connections and initiate church-planting activities.